For Linda —

A first-class spokeswoman for the Women's Bar and a dedicated attorney.

Best wishes in your continued activities on both fronts.

Sincerely,

Emily Couric

Oct. 1984

WOMEN LAWYERS

Perspectives on Success

WOMEN LAWYERS

Perspectives on Success

edited by Emily Couric

LAW & BUSINESS, INC./HARCOURT BRACE JOVANOVICH, PUBLISHERS

Permissions, Law & Business, Inc.
757 Third Avenue, New York, N.Y. 10017

Printed in the United States of America

Library of Congress Cataloging in Publication Data

Main entry under title:

Women lawyers.

1. Lawyers—United States—Biography. 2. Women lawyers—United States—Biography. I. Couric, Emily.
KF372.W65 1983 349.73'092'4 [B] 83-22811
ISBN 0-15-004290-6 347.300924 [B]

This book is dedicated to the many women lawyers who have helped me in my job as a reporter and editor covering the legal profession.

ACKNOWLEDGMENTS

Stephen W. Seemer offered support and guidance with this book project. Nancy E. White was a valuable assistant in the editing process. Kathryn M. Silverio took great care in designing the book, and Kimberly Warren was an able proofreader.

CONTENTS

INTRODUCTION

BY EMILY COURIC

John Grant

EMILY COURIC

INTRODUCTION

There's a revolution going on in the legal profession. The change isn't taking place in the law itself, or in how the law is practiced, but in *who* is practicing it. That is, the law is no longer a field dominated by men. Women now account for almost 40 percent of all students entering law school today.

When they look to older role models, however, they find out exactly how recently the legal profession has changed to let women in great numbers enter its ranks. The mature, successful woman lawyer today, although her profession may be very dear to her, faced innumerable stumbling blocks along the way. And even the younger role model, who may seem fully integrated in the ranks of our nation's attorneys, can still point out challenges for women lawyers intermingled with their numerous accomplishments.

The purpose of this book is to offer a sampling of the different avenues women lawyers can follow today—through the perspectives of those who have successfully charted their own courses. The book is composed of very personal chapters written by women lawyers themselves, who were chosen simply based on their reputations for success.

* * *

When Joan Bernstein joined New York's Shearman & Sterling as an associate in 1951—freshly graduated from Yale Law School—a partner at the firm asked her to join him for lunch at one of the city's distinguished private clubs. Upon reaching the dining room, the maitre d' approached the couple with great chagrin and embarrassment. "You know, sir," he said to the Shearman & Sterling partner, "ladies are not permitted in the dining room."

Without blinking, Bernstein's host replied, "She's no lady. She's a lawyer." And so they went in.

* * *

More recently, Lois Wood, a legal services lawyer in the very poor and black neighborhood of East St. Louis, Ill., found herself working on behalf of the community to keep a hospital there open. The local Health Systems Agency's board of directors was meeting to approve the proposed closing, a prerequisite since the hospital was federally funded. That night, Wood made a statement before the board arguing that the hospital needed to stay open; she included as part of her remarks a finding by the Office of Civil Rights of the U.S. Department of Health and Human Services that there had been a civil rights violation. The white owners of the hospital had not in good faith tried to keep the hospital in operating condition, the government said, putting it in such bad shape that it would have to go out of business.

The board of directors voted against the closing.

Walking out of the meeting, the attorney representing the hospital owners said to the hospital's administrator, "Well, what do you expect to happen when that little girl stands up with tears in her eyes?"

In telling this story, Wood laughingly noted "I'm not little, and I'm not a girl, and I wasn't crying." The slight at her legal ability was overshadowed, however, when the owners subsequently gave the hospital to a new black-owned corporation and provided it with a $300,000 fund for improvements.

* * *

When it comes to the public's perception, women lawyers have had their problems. Back when Bernstein entered the profession, women weren't supposed to go to law school and enter such a "manly" field. (In fact, back then, people generally thought that women weren't supposed to work at all.) Those very few who did become attorneys were, therefore, by definition, considered by many to be unladylike. The fact that they were such a distinct minority made them even more open to public scrutiny and suspicion.

Yet as Wood's story points out, even though far more women have entered the legal profession, they are still viewed in many cases as "lady lawyers," while their male counterparts are simply "lawyers." Some still have trouble believing that women can be successful attorneys. Wood also related, for example, that once when she spoke at a public hearing, the photographer from the local newspaper took a picture of her which appeared in the newspaper the next day. The caption underneath read: "Lois Wood, who identified herself as an attorney."

* * *

In the 1982-83 school year, women comprised 36.8 percent of all persons in law school, the American Bar Association reported. That is, in the 172 schools accredited by the ABA, women accounted for 47,083 of the 127,828 students enrolled.

As is the case every year since the late 1960s, the 1982-83 percentage was an increase over the year before—up from 35.3 percent. Back in 1972, women had accounted for a mere 12 percent of all law students.

Concomitantly, the number of women attorneys is increasing. In 1970, according to the American Bar Foundation, 2.8 percent of all lawyers in this country were women; ten years later, in 1980, that percentage had jumped to just over eight. This was indeed a significant jump considering that for the previous two decades, from 1950 to 1970, the proportion of women in the legal profession hovered in the area of 2.5 to 2.8 percent.

Yet in 1980, 75 percent of the women lawyers were 40-years-old or younger. Their median age was only 32.

* * *

In no way is this collection intended to represent a sociological or scientific study of women lawyers. Yet, the authors' views are, understandably, divergent. Some wrote that they had minimal difficulty as women lawyers, others much more. The types of problems they encountered varied, of course, according to their personal goals, the nature of the jobs they took on, and the other demands in their daily lives, as well as to the point in time in which they entered the legal profession. Their responses to given situations have been molded in large part by the nature of their interactions with others (most often men) working around them.

The first four chapters are devoted to private practice. In Chapter One, Peggy Kerr, now a partner with New York's Skadden, Arps, Slate, Meagher & Flom, relates tales about her experiences as an associate in the high-pressure world of large corporate law firms. As she writes, "If one begins the practice of law as a 'terrific broad'—as opposed, for example, to being simply a 'terrific lawyer'—some of the accumulated memories are bound to be uniquely female." The first woman to make partner with Skadden, Arps, Kerr can recall now with some humor being sent out to get doughnuts for a meeting of male attorneys, and on another occasion being bullied by a judge during her first argument before a court of appeals, and she relates her own reactions to those situations. Yet she is also careful to point out in the beginning of her chapter that "there's little here of that which I love about the law and my niche in it, for that I have in common with any man who has walked the same road."

Joan Bernstein in Chapter Two tells of her career path after graduating from Yale Law School in 1951. After taking 15 years off to raise three children, Bernstein passed through a succession of government jobs (several of them high-level) and settled for practice as a partner with a large Washington, D.C.-based firm, Wald, Harkrader & Ross. It was because of her government career success, Bernstein recalls, that she had the opportunity to move into a large firm partnership. And, she adds, "the years in government demonstrated that my lifestyle and workstyle were much more compatible with a larger organization. Large firms can offer support advantages—professional and administrative—that small firms can't provide."

Nancy Buc in Chapter Three also explains how she elected to work in a large corporate law firm. Buc got her start with the federal government (where her boss at first said not to work nights or weekends because the neighborhood was unsafe for women), and while litigating a case, so impressed a private firm adversary that he later offered her a job. Buc's mentors at Weil, Gotshal & Manges "went to bat" for her repeatedly, knocking aside opposition to a woman lawyer. After making partner there, Buc was one of several women who moved into high-level legal posts with the Carter Administration (she became general counsel for the Food and Drug Administration). When the Republicans won the next election, she returned to Weil, Gotshal. Jumping between private practice and government is common in Washington, D.C., but Buc relates her experiences as a woman following the path traditionally dominated by upwardly mobile males. It was a path fraught with difficulty.

In Chapter Four, Marna Tucker extols the virtues she has found in a small firm partnership. "It has the advantage over a large firm," explains Tucker, "of allowing more intimate knowledge and appreciation of your partners and your business." She said that she more easily can "feel the responsibility, the sharing of burdens with my partners, and the pride." Yet none of these feelings came easily—Tucker struggled through some rough times lobbying her partners for maternity leave and the opportunity to go home two hours earlier than usual each day while she was nursing her baby. Although Tucker billed as many if not more hours than any of her partners the year she was nursing, they still insisted on docking her partnership share for the time she was not in the office. Since then her partners have become more accommodating. "I chose a small firm so I could impress my own values on it, and not simply have the firm impress its values on me," asserts Tucker.

Chapter Five relates Lois Wood's experiences as a legal services lawyer for the indigent. Having never planned to attend law school, even through the time of her college graduation, Wood discovered that she was awed by Harvard Law School (her husband had a post doctoral fellowship in Harvard's Biological Laboratories). "But as I met students there, I began to realize that they seemed neither brighter nor more articulate than I," recalls Wood. Her second year of law school, she worked at the Harvard Legal Aid Bureau, "and almost from the day I walked in the door," she explains, "I knew that I had found my career." In her chapter, Wood describes the kinds of work she handles as the head of a legal services office, and her own special blend of professional and personal life which has helped her avoid after nine years the "burn-out" so typical of others who spend time in legal services.

Marcia Greenberger chose a career as a public interest lawyer for "the chance to work full-time on issues of great importance." She joined the Center for Law and Social Policy in Washington, D.C. to work on women's rights—a move which lead to the founding of the Women's Rights Project, and nine years later, to the creation of an independent National Women's Law Center. At the Center, Greenberger works to ensure women's rights in numerous areas including education, employment, and income security (such as welfare benefits and social security). In that capacity today, she works closely with other women's groups, ranging from the National Organization for Women to the American Association of University Women. "Attention paid by the press to women's interests has heightened," writes Greenberger, "and Administration officials recognize the implications of women becoming a political force."

At the other end of the legal job spectrum, Catherine Rein explains in Chapter Seven the particular pleasure she finds in serving as the chief lawyer for a major corporation, The Continental Group. "While outside lawyers may never get to see their clients again, or the long-term effects of their legal advice, inside, you become part of a team and can take continuing pride in your contribution," writes Rein. She offers from her own experience tips on choosing the right corporation and climbing the corporate hierarchy. And she reflects on women's particular situation within a large company, commenting, for example, that "many women, myself included, have not defined career goals as well as men have learned to do."

Janet Reno, state attorney for Dade County, Fla., which encompasses the city of Miami, vividly describes in Chapter Eight the pressure cooker environment in which she operates. As the prosecutor in a jurisdiction of 26 different police agencies, a jurisdiction which has been troubled with violent crime, Reno has tried to maintain her own standards for working within the criminal justice system. She says that being a woman has had no effect on her handling of the job, yet, partially because she is a woman, the way in which she executes her responsibilities is continually under public scrutiny. Whatever the public response, Reno rises above others' opinions in her long-term view of the commitment: "I think it is our responsibility to look through the violence, gore, and fraud [the police agencies] deal with to understand why people commit crime; to look beyond the criminal justice system to other institutions that may have failed the criminal to see what can be done to prevent crime and to make the system better," she concludes.

Jo Ann Harris writes of her experience as a federal prosecutor in the job of executive assistant to the U.S. Attorney for the Southern District of New York. In Chapter Nine, Harris quickly credits her height (5' 11") and her voice (low-pitched) for making a significant contribution to her success in the law. They are "priceless in a trade which places a premium on command presence," she writes. Harris relates joyfully her discovery of a love for law—more specifically for being a trial lawyer—and her decision to become part of the criminal justice system. She also explains how she dealt with her concerns about being an older lawyer (she was 39 when she graduated from law school), because it was a greater worry to her than being female. Yet she is still troubled about the future of other women in the law. "It may very well be that the power which resides in a prosecutor's office has protected me and my colleagues from grosser forms of sex discrimination not easily overcome by hard work and competence," Harris concludes.

Chapter Ten is Anne Jones' story of a successful woman executive in the federal bureaucracy. She climbed her way to the top ranks of the Securities and Exchange Commission, to the general counsel's seat at the Federal Home Loan Bank Board, and then to a commissioner's slot with the Federal Communications Commission. Yet when Jones graduated from law school in 1961, she was overtly discriminated against when seeking a job with private law firms. "In later years I have sometimes been embarrassed that I was not one of the first to fight the system in the courts or in the legislature, but it simply never occurred to me," writes Jones. Instead, because of her search for "a more satisfying practice," she took advantage of opportunities in the government to accept a variety of management positions. Her chapter is a detailed account of the type of work these positions involved and the career choices she made in shifting from one to another.

Yvonne Burke is a political lawyer. Chapter Eleven includes her experiences in the California State Legislature and in the U.S. House of Representatives. Being a lawyer was important for these elections, Burke explains: "It didn't matter whether the candidate was a woman or a man—if he or she was an 'attorney' the public assumed that the credentials were there for the job." In her chapter, Burke also analyzes women's ability to function in the political arena, including their skills in forming close political alliances and in raising campaign funds.

Chapter Twelve is Dorothy Nelson's contribution as a federal judge. She tells of her road to success through academia, which gave her the opportunity to build a reputation while still attending to traditional family needs. Nelson's position as dean of the University of Southern California Law Center made her a visible candidate for a seat on the U.S. Court of Appeals for the Ninth Circuit. Partially influencing her decision to accept the post was a belief that "until women attain high policy-making positions, the very peace of the world is at stake." Nelson believes that a woman's own unique qualities are necessary for balanced leadership.

Lillian BeVier in Chapter Thirteen details the three responsibilities of a law professor: teaching, scholarship, and "collegiality." She tries to describe the pressure points in her own career "that seemed to me to come from being a woman," thinking that "perhaps that will help identify issues that might be of special concern to women law teachers generally." Despite the stresses of seeking tenure, BeVier can say that law teaching still doesn't carry the same pressures of private practice. "I get to think about things that *I* think are interesting rather than spending time worrying about whichever client's problem happens to be on the top of the pile on my desk," BeVier explains. "I also like having a working schedule almost entirely my own."

The flip side of the coin, Barbara Moses writes in Chapter Fourteen from the vantage point of a female law student. At Harvard Law School in the early 1980s, Moses found that discrimination, although much more subtle than in years past, still ran rampant. "Because of the absence of overt, shameless prejudice against women, it took me some time to discover the larger, more elusive problems still facing women at Harvard," she writes. Moses mentions systemic barriers such as admission criteria and trivial harassment as hurdles she discovered. The law school system, she argues, will not be free of such hindrances until women themselves alter some of the traditional criteria for judging performance and success.

And, finally, in Chapter Fifteen, Donna Fossum, a lawyer and a sociologist, presents an overview of women's past achievement in the legal profession. She, like Moses, has found that acceptance of women by the legal profession is "still quite grudging." Fossum predicts that by the year 2000, women will account for one third of all lawyers, but "unfortunately," she concludes, "even today, women's position within the legal profession, as well as society as a whole, is all too frequently that of visitor rather than member in full standing."

Should the percentage of women in law school continue to rise—say until it reflects women's proportion in the general population of about 50 percent—it could be expected that the population of working lawyers would eventually reflect the same ratio. Whether this will actually happen, however, no one can say. Perhaps the widely reported overabundance of attorneys will discourage increased enrollment in a profession recently opened to women, although some would argue that this should have no disproportionate effect on women as compared to men.

With the growing number of women lawyers, the profession has also witnessed a trend toward women trying to balance career and family. Not all women becoming attorneys today are ready to agree to a total abstinence from personal commitments as did many of those who excelled years ago as a distinct minority in a male-dominated world. Perhaps the pendulum will continue to swing away from the 1960s and 1970s women's rights explosion which thrust so many into law school and the profession, and more women will choose part-time options rather than the "either-family-or-job" choice previously thought so necessary. If part-time lawyering does catch on, women's representation in the world of working lawyers will undeniably be lessened.

Of course, all such discussion is mere speculation. The only certainty about the future of women in the legal profession is that they are increasingly exercising their right to choose whether to attend law school and to enter the law.

Exactly how they choose to go about using their law degrees in the decades to come remains to be seen. The options are plentiful and varied, and the track record of women along each career path—whether that be government service, private practice, or law teaching, for example—is steadily improving. Thus the examples for young women to follow are multiplying.

Let us hope that with the variety of role models offered through these chapters, other women will be even more adept at making inroads into the profession. Surely newcomers to the law eventually will be able to say that it's a club of wide opportunity, with membership open to all.

Emily Couric, Editor
Charlottesville, Virginia
January 1984

CHAPTER 1

AS BIG FIRM ASSOCIATE: War Stories to Laugh, or Cry, About

BY PEGGY L. KERR

Myra Alperson

PEGGY L. KERR

PEGGY L. KERR

Skadden, Arps, Slate, Meagher & Flom
New York, N.Y.

Education

J.D., University of Chicago Law School, 1973; "Best Overall Advocate," 1972-1973 and 1971-1972; Hinton Moot Court Finals, 1973; Karl N. Llewellyn Memorial Cup, 1972

A.B., The George Washington University, 1968, with special honors (American thought and civilization)

Experience

Partner, Skadden, Arps, Slate, Meagher & Flom, New York, N.Y., 1981-present

Associate, Skadden, Arps, Slate, Meagher & Flom, June 1973-December 1980

Summer Associate, Schiff, Hardin & Waite, Chicago, Ill., summer, 1972

Legal Assistant, Federal Defender Program, Chicago, Ill., summer, 1971

Equal Employment Officer, U.S. Equal Employment Opportunity Commission, Chicago, Ill., Nov. 1969-Oct. 1970

Management Intern, U.S. Equal Employment Opportunity Commission, Washington, D.C. and Chicago, Ill., Nov. 1968-Nov. 1969

Professional Activities

Admitted to practice in New York, 1974

Member, Association of the Bar of the City of New York

Member, Council of New York Law Associates

Member, Visiting Committee, University of Chicago Law School

Personal

Born: July 5, 1946, Libertyville, Ill.

Single

Children: One, adopted in 1983

Chapter 1

AS BIG FIRM ASSOCIATE: WAR STORIES TO LAUGH, OR CRY, ABOUT

BY PEGGY L. KERR

From the outset, there was little doubt that my experience of being an associate at a large firm was going to be somewhat different from the experience of my male colleagues. When I came to New York for a day's worth of interviews with Skadden, Arps, Slate, Meagher & Flom, the firm whose job offer I accepted and of which I later became the first woman partner, I noticed that the interviewing attorneys were giggling at my resume. Finally I asked one of them what was so funny. He handed me his copy of my resume, bearing the notations of the partner who had come to my law school to recruit. "A terrific broad," the recruiting partner had written, "a real bomb-thrower!"

There is a temptation to tell the ensuing 10 years as a succession of "war stories"—engrossing cases I have handled, clients I have known and liked and laughed at, judges and adversaries and co-counsel with their own amusing peculiarities, briefs to which I have touched my gold-tipped pen, arguments to which I have applied my gold-tongued oratory, intellectual challenges I have met and mastered. By and large, though, my war stories are not so terribly different in quality from those of my male colleagues. I, too, started in the library. I have worked the same long hours as they, the same nights and weekends; I have worked on roughly the same kinds of cases, with at least as much responsibility and client contact. There's not one of us, male or female, who doesn't have a vignette to tell along the lines of being in three different cities before three different judges seeking or opposing three different temporary restraining orders in one 24 hour period.

Still, if one begins the practice of law as a "terrific broad"—as opposed, for example, to being simply a "terrific lawyer"—some of the accumulated memories are bound to be uniquely female. Not all are bad, but retelling others is more like poking at war wounds than entertaining the recruits with war stories. I have chosen in this chapter to tell some anecdotes that strike me as relating to the woman's experience of my professional world, but in doing so, I recognize the risk of giving a false impression. There's little here of that which I love about the law and my niche in it, for that I have in common with any man who has walked the same road. But no man has ever been asked to leave the lobby of the University Club, while waiting with a colleague for another lawyer to join them for a business lunch, on the ground that "ladies aren't allowed in the lobby, sir."

Nor, for that matter, do men generally have to worry about being taken for a secretary. Not long after I had started at my firm, I was working on a Saturday in an "annex" to the library. We were smaller then—70 lawyers, perhaps, as opposed to the more than 300 of today—and telephone-answering was often a catch-as-catch-can affair on Saturdays; whoever was most irritated by the screech of the outside bell caved in and answered the phone.

A boy of 13 or 14 poked his head into the library annex and said, a touch haughtily, "My father says that someone should answer the phone."

"Who is your father?" I asked

"Joe Flom," came the answer.

Oh. Joe Flom, then as now, was a man surrounded by legend, the acknowledged master of the corporate takeover, seen even by many of his partners as ever so slightly larger than life and certainly by his associates as an intimidating figure.

"Well," said I to the boy, "there's a secretary on the other side of the floor. I'll call her and make sure she's answering the phone." Which I did.

As the boy trotted off, I walked out to the nearby secretarial desk where the weekend mail used to be dumped. Joe Flom was standing there, going through his mail.

"Hi," I said, holding out my hand; "I'm Peggy Kerr. I've just started here as an associate." Joe and I chatted briefly. A few minutes later, after I'd gone back to the library annex, I overheard a father-son conversation that ended like this: "You know that lady you first met? She's not a secretary; she's a lawyer."

It may well have been that incident that led me to indulge freely in my habit of drafting on a typewriter, without fear that it would diminish my status. A client called once and said, "You must be a very secure woman lawyer." Why did he think that? "Because you have a typewriter in your office," he answered, "and you *use* it."

Certainly my early years of practice suggested no reasons for insecurity about my role as a woman in law. There were awkward situations, of course, but for every one of those, there was another that could easily have given me a swollen head.

During my first year out of law school, I was assigned to handle, with local counsel, a series of securities fraud cases in a small city about two hours from New York. The first time I went there for a court appearance, I met local counsel at the coffee shop across the street from the courthouse, where he and a significant percentage of the local bar met for breakfast every morning. He introduced me to his breakfast companions as "Peggy Kerr, the big New York lawyer." It was in connection with those cases, one of which was a class action brought in federal court, that I had an experience few first-year, big firm associates, male or female, can claim: essentially single-handedly, I briefed and argued a motion to dismiss the federal securities claims on their merits.

Because of such heady experiences, I may have been slower than many to figure out that the legal profession was not universally populated by Sir Walter Raleighs, all standing ready to lay down their cloaks to protect my dainty feet from the mud. One of my more pointed lessons came in the context of some litigation that was being conducted both in Canada and in New York on which I had worked for three often frenetic years. The Canadian piece of the litigation was on appeal to the Supreme Court of Canada. I had expected, and the clients had expected, that I would be in Ottawa to see the argument.

The Canadian lawyers, however, had taken responsibility for making hotel reservations, and they had deliberately failed to make one for me. As it was explained to me, one of the Canadian lawyers was very "old school," and he didn't like being around women who say "shit." Therefore I couldn't go to Ottawa where he would be. His New York counterparts, to their undying discredit, found the explanation credible, cogent, logical, and perfectly acceptable. Never mind the fact that any man in the world is free to say "shit" without penalty. Because there was no available hotel room by the time I found out I was being excluded, I did not attend the argument.

I wouldn't want it to be thought that New Yorkers are any less guilty of male chauvinism than are Canadians. I was litigating a precedent-setting case in a midwestern city about five years ago with a partner from my firm, Logan, and two younger associates—Don, who was about three years out of law school, and Mary, who had just graduated. Our co-counsel was a renowned New York litigating attorney, fond of foul-smelling cigars, who thought that the funniest thing in the world was to tell women lawyers to their faces that they were supposed to be barefoot or pregnant or both. Every conference room he inhabited had a locker-room quality to it.

I had grimly tolerated his tasteless brand of humor until, as I was going out to lunch with Mary one day, he asked me to bring him back some doughnuts. "Look," I exploded, "let's get one thing straight. I'm not a secretary, and I'm not a waitress, and I'm not a messenger. I'm a lawyer. As far as you're concerned, I write briefs. I do not go out for doughnuts."

"Hey! What are you getting excited about?" he responded. "You're going out for lunch, right? If you should *happen* to pass a place that sells doughnuts on your way back, would you be so kind as to bring a dozen of them back, as a courtesy to a fellow lawyer?"

Realizing that, for anyone else, I probably wouldn't have blinked twice about performing such a service, I brought the man back a dozen doughnuts, for which he graciously thanked me.

The next day, at about lunch time, I found a note from him in the office where I was working: "You did such a good job yesterday that I know I can trust you to bring back another dozen doughnuts today." So much for trying to treat a confirmed male chauvinist pig like a human being.

In that same case, we had wooed and won the expert witness services of an academic luminary, a living legend in his field, whom I'll call Albert Einstein. This particular Einstein was not an altogether charming person, tending toward the arrogant. More seriously, as we prepared him for his testimony, it developed that, although he had much to say in support of the proposition we were trying to prove, he had some other things to say that were decidedly harmful to our case. The group of us walked back to the office after dinner, lawyers troubled of mind and expert witness, seeming to enjoy himself ever so much, singing, "Oh My Darling, Clementine."

The next morning Logan's instructions to Don and Mary were, "Keep Einstein in the office." As Logan and I sat in court, Mary came to report that Einstein was getting increasingly excited about testifying, even calling the library for books and articles that he might be able to cite. "Send him back to his hotel room," barked Logan.

A little later, Mary returned to the courtroom to tell Logan, "He's already checked out of his hotel room." While Logan was chewing over that news, Mary whispered to me: "Don says to tell Logan that if he wants Albert Einstein fired, he can goddamned well do it himself." Logan's solution to the problem was to instruct Mary: "Tell him that we'll have a plane meet him, and he should go back home."

But for the slightest quiver of her lip, Mary froze. I looked at Mary, Mary looked at me; I looked at Logan, Logan looked at me. To me, basic fairness suggested that Don was right: if Logan wanted Albert Einstein fired, Logan should do it himself, and he certainly shouldn't delegate the task to someone no more than four months out of law school. But Logan was either of a different mind or too cowardly to do his own dirty work. Finally, I said to Logan, "Do you want me to go back to the office and do it?" "Um-Hmmm," he answered.

Sure enough, back at the office, Einstein was madly reviewing the literature in his field. He leapt upon the opportunity to try a few testimonial facts out on me. "Uh," I started, "we have been thinking that perhaps your testimony might not be necessary, and it's a shame for you to have to sit around like this."

"Oh, I don't mind staying," Einstein replied brightly.

"Well, uh," groped I, "we're actually a little concerned that, even though they aren't really inconsistent, some of the facts you'll talk about may *sound* inconsistent with other testimony we're putting in."

"Oh, that's no problem. I can explain that."

"Look," I began again, "it's just that we think that, without meaning to, you could do actual damage to our case, and . . . ."

The man looked as if he'd been hit with a baseball bat. "I wouldn't want to hurt your case; I didn't come here for that."

So I told him that we had a private jet waiting for him. I told him an always-a-bridesmaid-never-a-bride story, and he told me an always-a-bridesmaid-never-a-bride story. I collared my two younger associates so that all of us would form an honor guard to walk Professor Einstein to a cab. He departed with a kiss for each of the ladies.

I went back upstairs to wait a decent interval before returning to the courtroom where Einstein was forbidden. After half an hour or so, when I was calmer, I decided that the coast was probably clear. Walking out of the office building, however, I ran smack dab into Professor Einstein—blood on his nose, tears in his eyes. He'd waited for a cab for a half an hour, and in his distress he had walked into a glass door on his way back upstairs to call a taxi.

That afternoon after court, Logan was gloating. "The best thing that's happened to me in two and a half years as a partner is making somebody else fire Albert Einstein," he crowed. He wasn't remarkably understanding, either, when, after a couple of glasses of dinner wine, I started to cry.

There was one more time when the stresses of work caused me to cry publicly, and I was convinced at the time that I had done irreparable damage to my career. A team of us had worked straight through one weekend and all Sunday night, preparing a set of papers so that an unappreciative and personally unpleasant client could commence a lawsuit on Monday in a distant state. Aside from the complaint, there were eight accompanying documents—all drafted that one mad weekend, while the client kept calling to insult our judgment and our work.

After a younger associate, Bill, got on an early Monday morning plane to take the papers to local counsel for signature, I went home to bed. A couple of hours later, I was roused from heavy sleep by Bill, calling long distance: "Local counsel doesn't want to sign the papers."

"WHAT!!!!"

"Don't be upset, Peggy. It's not so bad. It's just that he believes that Defendant X is guiltier than Defendant Y, so he wants to add a five-word phrase in the complaint and reverse the order of the first two names in the caption."

In despair that somebody else's theory of the case—no more valid than mine—might cause the retyping of *nine* separate litigation documents and delay filing by an additional day, I called the partner in charge, Paul, who had a long-standing friendship with the local counsel causing the trouble.

"Can't you control your friend well enough so that we don't have to change the captions on nine papers?" I demanded.

"If he can't sign the complaint, then he can't sign the complaint," Paul yelled back in my ear.

"If he can't sign the complaint because he doesn't like the order of the names in the caption, then he deserves to retype all nine papers himself!" And in exasperation, I slammed down the telephone in Paul's ear.

A minute later, he called back. "Look," he said, placatingly, "you don't have to come in to do it."

By this time, I was crying. "Who will do it then?" I sobbed.

"Terry Bright's still here," he answered; "I'll have her do it."

"But Terry Bright was there all weekend with me," I sobbed. "She hasn't had any more sleep than I have."

The matter was taken care of, somehow, while I slept. And I noticed the next day that the captions had remained unchanged.

There were, however, a few more obstacles and delays in getting the papers filed. The following day, Bill, who, on top of having had no sleep, was undergoing the frustrations of dealing with local counsel and the client, called in with some problems to discuss. He was at the client's offices and had gone into a separate room to call Paul.

Over the speakerphone in the partner's office came Bill's emotionally wrought voice: "Goddammit, Paul," *he* sobbed. "Take me off that fucking speakerphone." Thus was I redeemed for the unpardonable female sin of crying in front of a partner by the like sin of my male colleague.

I haven't yet cried in court, although I've certainly felt like it on occasion. While still a law student, I had been told by seasoned female practitioners that they had known a time when judges tended to bend over backwards to be gentlemanly when confronted with the rare creature in skirts who graced their courtrooms. That era, if ever it was, passed me by. With a single exception, I have known from judges neither greater nor lesser courtesy than my male colleagues report.

The one exception, however, left some bruises. It was my first argument before the Second Circuit Court of Appeals. I was especially honored by—and nervous about—doing the argument because it was at the specific request of two of the several clients we represented in the case, both elderly lawyers themselves. They had taken an interest in my professional development and wanted me to have the chance to argue.

Presiding on that fateful day was a distinguished jurist with a long and admirable career behind him and sickness and death before him. He in fact died not long after. At issue was whether a lower court's disapproval of a settlement of a derivative action was sufficiently "final" to be immediately appealable. At the time, the only precedent held that it was.

The presiding judge did not care much for my argument that the precedent was sound and should be followed. Either that, or he didn't hear it. Barely two sentences were out of my mouth when he growled, "Speak up, young lady; you're mumbling." Naturally, I raised my voice and continued my argument.

"Speak up. Speak up, young lady," the judge demanded.

I tried again, several decibels louder still, but to no avail. In utter exasperation, the judge said, "Young lady, you have to speak up. Say . . . every . . . word . . . slowly . . . and . . . distinctly . . . just . . . like . . . I'm . . . talking . . . now."

Having "young lady-ed" me to the point of mortification, the judge proceeded to deepen the day's humiliation. After a brief recess (during which my colleagues reassured me that I had been neither mumbling nor whispering), the court returned to announce from the bench that I had lost and that it was dismissing the appeal.

It was a long time before I could look back on that day without wincing. It helped, though, that a couple of years later, the identical issue came before the U.S. Supreme Court, which overruled the decision in my case, holding that an order disapproving a settlement of a class or derivative action *is* an appealable order. At that, I stopped sticking mental pins into an effigy of the deceased appellate judge and let him rest easy in his grave.

The day after that disastrous argument, I arranged to have lunch with a partner who had always been a booster of mine, hoping he would find words of comfort and encouragement to salve my bruised ego. It was not to be. Indeed, it seemed as if the judge's hostility on the prior day had been a declaration of open season on "young ladies." My problem, I was told, was that I kept doing all sorts of unabashedly female things. I had once cried, for instance (little did he know I'd actually cried *twice* in my career). Principal among my sins was that, four or five years earlier, when I was a first-year associate at my first firm "prom," I had had the temerity to ask a very senior partner to dance.

"I'm not telling you not to act like a woman," he said; "I'm just telling you to act like the women who've succeeded."

But who are they? And do they dance, or cry, or argue in the Second Circuit?

Probably they don't go to Christmas parties, for his final words to me, most ominous of all, were: "If John Smith gets drunk at the Christmas party, nobody will even notice, but if Peggy Kerr gets drunk at the Christmas party, they'll remember it forever."

No one should have to live under the constant fear that a single indiscretion—one tantrum, one drink too many, one crying bout, one scatological comment—could permanently damage her professional future. And if one must live under that sort of pressure at work, at least there ought to be someone or something at home to counterbalance the strain. The irony, of course, is that the greater the pressures at work are, the less likely it is that there will be anything at home except a lot of unread magazines and a neglected cat.

It is surely clear by now that an associate's life at a big firm, at least at *my* big firm, is not a 9-to-5 existence. It doesn't require the commitment of every night and every weekend by any means, but the schedule one will have to work is unpredictable: a fascinating, demanding, exhilarating crisis may be followed by a lull, only to be followed by a crisis that is only demanding, not fascinating or exhilarating. What makes it worthwhile is that there are far more of the fascinating crises than the boring ones.

It is nonetheless very hard on one's personal life. I have a hunch, shared by my female colleagues, that men are more credible than are women when they cancel an evening's plans because, "I'm sorry, honey, but I have to work." The man who will put up with being told by his ladylove, five times in a row, "I'm sorry, honey, but I have to work," is simply not to be found.

There are, of course, ways to work around this problem. I can't count the number of times I've ducked out of the office, leaving a team behind, to have dinner with a man, only to return to the office for as long as necessary until I could rejoin him—at 2 or 3 or 4 in the morning.

And colleagues do step in to cover for you when necessary. Once I had planned to take a romantic week in Paris at the Hotel Ritz with the man in my life when I was commandeered into working on a major litigated corporate takeover. I was perfectly happy to go anywhere I was needed, to do anything I could, to put in all-nighters every night, provided it didn't interfere with my Paris tryst. So I jetted about the country, handled a hearing, wrote a few briefs, lost a lot of sleep and made my plane to France.

While I was gone, one of the lawyers from the other side, having failed to reach me, called the partner in charge of the case. He asked where I was and was told I was in Paris.

"You mean you let her go on vacation in the middle of a tender offer?" the lawyer said, with mock horror.

"I had to," the partner said. "It's good for recruiting."

Even if time can be managed, a big firm lawyer seems to suffer other disadvantages in the market for dates and mates. At the most recent of the annual parties I give for my women associates, we tried to figure out how many women had married men they'd met after they'd started working at the firm. Since there are 60 or more of us now, we were looking back on at least 100 women, perhaps 150, over the past 10 years. Plenty of them are married, but the basic rule seems to be that either you're married when you start, or you marry the man you were already engaged to or living with, or you stay single. We could think of only two exceptions to that rule.

There's no way to know how many men I didn't get to know better because I was too busy with, or too enthralled by, my work to be able to give it up, even temporarily, for him. I do know that I lost at least one.

Peter was an attorney, too, and a gifted one. We'd met at a continuing legal education seminar. Throughout the relationship there had been a concern that we'd find ourselves competing with, or trying to one-up, one another. The "competition" problem was trivial, as it turned out, and was certainly outweighed by the pleasures of being able to talk to someone who really understood what my work was all about.

One night, out of the blue, he called a pow-wow to break off the relationship. "I want to get married," he explained, "so I should only be dating women I could marry."

My eyes must have widened, for I hadn't really understood that I was so terribly inappropriate. Then he spelled it out: "You're a lawyer." It was that simple. "I can't marry a lawyer," he said.

He was attracted, you see, to women who were smart and high-powered and successful. But eventually they were supposed to give up whatever else they were doing and devote themselves full-time to being a "cheerleader" for him and caretaker of his children.

"I could never ask you to give up the law," he insisted. "I wouldn't *let* you give it up; you're too good at it."

His logic was eluding me, so I pointed out that people, including women, have spouses and children and jobs, too.

"Let's face it, Peggy," he said, in one of the cruelest accusations ever hurled, "your children will have the best mothering money can buy."

I have no children yet to mother myself or to buy mothering for. Anyone who has been in my office—decorated with my photographs of children, drawings by my nieces and nephews and godchildren, and at least half a dozen toys—would suspect that I mean to change that condition at the earliest opportunity. A partner bearing just such a suspicion stopped by my office one day to invite me to lunch. Thinking he was on a "morale" trip through the associates, I gladly accepted.

Lunch was delightful and useful, as well. I was having some difficulty with a boyfriend at the time, largely because his mother didn't like me. I pumped this partner, who has daughters my age, for information and insights about parents' attitudes toward their children's boy/girlfriends and how to handle them (if at all).

Socializing, as it turned out, had not been the sole purpose of the lunch, nor was giving me advice on how to deal with my boyfriend's mother. By the time we got to coffee, the partner coughed nervously and said, "Do you mind if I ask you a personal question?"

"Well," I answered, "I don't know. Why don't you ask it, and if I don't want to answer it, I won't."

"Uh," he began, "uh . . . are you pregnant?"

Not a little taken aback, since I hadn't even gained any weight recently, I gulped twice and answered, "No . . . but why do you ask?"

"Oh," he rushed to say, "somebody told me, but I'll just tell him it's crazy, he's crazy."

"It's not crazy," I answered thoughtfully, "but I'm not pregnant."

"You mean . . ." he started, brightening with vindication and relief, "you mean you had an abortion?"

Well, no, that wasn't what I meant either.

Neither of us was ever able to track down the source of the rumor. He'd taken me to lunch, though, believing me both pregnant and just bull-headed enough to bear a child on my own, as a single woman. His self-imposed mission had been to convince me that it wasn't such a good idea and could jeopardize my career.

Single motherhood unquestionably would have jeopardized my career, but so would married motherhood. To my mind, it is no accident that the three most senior women in my firm have either never married or were divorced long ago, and all are childless. I have no doubt that, had I had the wonderful husband and two adorable children I thought I wanted years ago, I would not be a partner today.

Maybe things would be different if I had started a few years later, after certain trails were already blazed. The first lawyer in the firm ever to become visibly pregnant did so in the midst of putting together a major corporate acquisition. Recognizing that her services were essential to the transaction, the senior lawyers on the deal carefully calculated the scheduled closing date of the acquisition in relation to the due date of the child, heaving a sigh of relief when the former preceded the latter by a month.

Still a little worried, they inquired whether the woman would be able to work full tilt right up to the closing date. She, who was feeling fine, replied that she could. "But," she added, "I really need at least one day off every week."

The senior lawyers were stunned. "You mean you only want to work four days a week?" one said, unable to hide the disapproval in his voice.

"Oh, no," she laughed. "I mean I need either Saturday *or* Sunday off."

Nowadays, there's a great deal of tolerance for associates who are also mothers, and who want to work part-time or in the less demanding specialties, but, even now, their road to partnership is correspondingly lengthened—if, indeed, they will ever see the end of it.

As for me, after seven and a half years, I came to the end of my road as an associate. I learned that I had just been named the first woman partner in the history of the firm.

The tradition is that, on the morning after the meeting in which new partners have been elected, all the old partners gather in the office of founding partner Leslie Arps. They then summon the newcomers (who are supposed to be surprised), and Les announces the new partners.

It was clear on this particular morning that we'd all changed in small but significant measure. I, for example, was no longer "a real bomb-thrower." And Les did a slight editing job on his remarks: "Since the memory of *a person* runneth not to the contrary," he said, "it has been my pleasure to announce the new partners."

We agreed that one of the nicer aspects of the changes was that, for the first time, there was a partner who, when joyous, could kiss her partners in public.

CHAPTER 2

AS PARTNER IN A LARGE FIRM:
The Joy of Collegiality

BY JOAN Z. BERNSTEIN

Julie Wiatt

JOAN Z. BERNSTEIN

JOAN Z. BERNSTEIN

Wald, Harkrader & Ross
Washington, D.C.

Education

LL.B., Yale Law School, 1951; Phi Kappa Phi; Board of Editors, *Yale Law Journal*

B.A., University of Wisconsin, 1948 (economics)

Experience

Partner, Wald, Harkrader & Ross, Washington, D.C., 1981-present

General Counsel, Department of Health and Human Services, Washington, D.C., 1979-1981

General Counsel, Environmental Protection Agency, Washington, D.C., 1977-1979

Partner, Baker & Hostetler, Washington, D.C., 1976-1977

Trial Attorney, Assistant to Director, Acting Director, Deputy Director, Acting Director, Federal Trade Commission, 1970-1976

Associate, William B. Wolf, Jr., Washington, D.C., 1968-1970

Associate, Dahlstream, Schiff, Waite & Hardin, Chicago, Ill., 1952-1953

Associate, Shearman & Sterling, New York, N.Y., 1951-1952

Professional Activities

Admitted to practice in New York, 1951; *in Illinois,* 1952; *in the District of Columbia,* 1969

Appointed by the President to the Council of the Administrative Conference of the United States, September 1978; Appointed Vice Chairman, June 1980

Appointed by the President to the Commission on Wartime Relocation and Internment of Civilians, January 1981; Elected Chairman, February 1981

Council Member, Administrative Law Section, American Bar Association, April 1981

Appointed Chair, Education Committee, Administrative Law Section, ABA, April 1981

Member, Standing Committee on Environmental Law, ABA, 1978-1979

EPA Representative to Administrative Conference, prior to appointment to the Council

Government Representative to the Litigation Section of the ABA, 1980

Elected Member of the Executive Committee, Yale Law School, for a term of four years, October 1980

Chairman, Consumer Protection Committee, Antitrust Section of the ABA, 1973-1977

Personal

Born: March 17, 1926, Galesburg, Ill.

Married: 1953

Children: Three, born in 1956, 1957, and 1962

Chapter 2

AS PARTNER IN A LARGE LAW FIRM: THE JOY OF COLLEGIALITY

BY JOAN Z. BERNSTEIN

Current and future prospects for women lawyers in big city, big firm law practice may best be appreciated by looking at our past. Some say "we've come a long way, baby"—and in many ways we have. Deciding just how far, in other words taking a retrospective review, may help to get a perspective on where we are today and where we may be tomorrow.

I represent a miniscule group of women of my generation—I have been a lawyer for 30 years. While we are a tiny group, we still had common experiences which may provide insight for assessing today's status of women in the profession and for predicting the future. A retrospective of my own career is somewhat typical of these pre-women's movement legal careers. My first jobs in the early 1950s were with big firms, an experience shared with many men who attended national law schools. I have spent considerable time in the government, which also is not an unusual career path. I served at several agencies in both career and political positions. In between these jobs, I took time off to raise a family.

In 1951, graduation from Yale Law School did not automatically produce job opportunities for women. Many law firms and other potential employers simply said they didn't hire women lawyers, "period." No reasons, no guilty expressions . . . it was just not done. Indeed, some whom I had the temerity to approach seemed annoyed that one might be expected to do anything so peculiar. There had been some "necessity" hiring of women lawyers during World War II, but that was considered mostly aberrant. Occasionally, a potential employer would recount a positive experience with a "lady lawyer," saying that "she thought like a man." I can recall trying to figure out how to demonstrate to potential employers that I could "think like a man." I never came up with anything except a random obscenity, which luckily I suppressed. No matter how absurd the inquiry seemed to the employer, most of us left these encounters at least vaguely convinced that we had failed personally. The burden of proof needed to overcome the adverse presumption was definitely on us.

Notwithstanding this general attitude—and to my astonishment—I was hired by Shearman & Sterling, then Wall Street's biggest, and one of its most establishment firms. I suspect that many in the firm were equally astonished to discover a woman among the entering group of white male legal stars. I did have at least one thing in common with my classmates: We were all terrified that we would not measure up, either in performance or in "fitting in."

I knew how high the standards were for performance. I wasn't exactly sure what constituted "fitting in." But it was evident, though formally unstated, that to become a partner one had not only to do first class legal work but also to meet the conformity criterion. The associates tried to observe how to look and behave like the successful people in the firm. I was not quite sure how to pattern myself because the successes on Wall Street were all men. For example, the men had to dress in the uniform—conservative pin stripe suits, vests, and ties, preferably "old school." The equivalent for me, I was told, was a hat and gloves. I never understood the "hat" rationale since I took it off when I arrived in the morning.

Once I took it off, however, equalization seemed to set in. I received the same types of assignments, worked the same excrutiating number of hours a week, and went home on the subway, no matter what hour, just as the male associates did. Mind you, such treatment was unusual for women. For the most part, women in law firms were not assigned to antitrust, bankruptcy, or general corporate work. The lack of opportunity in those fields was significant for many reasons, but primarily because lawyers who didn't get the "sexy" work didn't have a chance of making partner.

As to those prospects, a possible partnership was too far off to think about. We groveled along, obeying the associate "class" rules like not fraternizing with secretaries. The first year crowd only wanted to survive that year, get a bonus, and not make fools of ourselves at the firm Christmas party!

Although my brief description sounds incredible by today's standards, I did not feel in any way mistreated. Indeed, I was thrilled to be there, to have comparable work assignments, and to have the comradery of my colleagues. It is only with hindsight that I or others recall the uncertainty of trying to function in a totally male world.

When I moved to Chicago to a LaSalle Street law firm, Dahlstream, Schiff, Waite and Hardin, the code of conduct was even stricter and more clearly defined. Lawyers did not socialize at all with secretaries; for example, it was thought to be unprofessional and to create problems if these men lawyers and women secretaries ate lunch together. Although no rule was articulated to cover a female lawyer and lunch, the lack of a ruling resulted in my exclusion from the group of associates who then ate regularly together. I can recall feeling lonely and excluded, and part of an environment that didn't make sense. I did not complain because I felt lucky to be working in such a prestigious firm, and I thought that if I made waves, I would be even less acceptable.

I knew I had an opportunity that other women didn't have, and increasingly I became aware that no matter what I did, I would be regarded within my profession as something of an oddity. And I gradually realized that to go to the top of the ladder I would have to pay an extraordinary price because the view from where I was revealed that the women in the field (1) were not partners and (2) were primarily in positions where they produced on paper and were not let out of the office. Their heads were used but they never got to see anybody. Women were isolated—they were expected to be spinsters who lived extremely cloistered lives. The prevailing attitude was that there were to be tolerated a few of these eccentric, unattractive females who persisted in pursuing careers instead of husbands and children. All of us foolish enough to continue were suppressed, repressed, and powerless.

Society dictated that a woman unmarried had no place and was a failure. It was not a matter of choice. If a woman, lawyer or not, was unmarried, it was assumed no one had asked her and, therefore, she worked. Nobody who wanted to be successful in America in the 1950's would choose to be single. Indeed, at 25, my unmarried friends and I were nervous. Most of us knew that children would mean withdrawing from the profession for some time, maybe forever. Although I was concerned about career goals, I was not willing to be forever considered a slightly eccentric maiden lady lawyer who was never quite socially acceptable. I opted for the conventional.

I married, had three children, and moved several times, finally to Washington, D.C. I became a full-time housewife and mother who thought occasionally about resuming my career but discarded the idea because potential jobs were either boring, unrewarding, or unavailable. These also were still the years of "Young lady, you belong at home with your children!"

The time passed, and in 1968 the children seemed to be at a point where I could try to be a lawyer again. But when I thought about it after all that time, I felt absolutely desperate. I felt I could not possibly do anything—that my skills, obtained through so much effort, were gone, and that despite Betty Friedan's historic epic, things had not changed so much that a woman lawyer would be in any sort of demand. There still were almost no women in the profession, there still were people who "didn't hire women," and I was hardly a hot ticket, being middle-aged and out-of-date!

The fact that many of my male classmates were already partners in the best law firms in the country made me feel by comparison even more a failure. The sense of total failure nearly paralyzed me. I was nearly too embarrassed to go downtown! I only managed to emerge at all with the help and support of a few close friends, one of whom was reentering the work force at the same time. Some helped by reassuring me that I could recover my legal mind and by cheering me on. A law school classmate hired me to join his solo practice and permitted no indulgence. He threw me in to sink or swim, and after several near drownings, I began to relearn and recover my confidence.

My husband was also very supportive. Nevertheless, we bumped precariously through the transition. It's one thing to say "Yes, of course, my wife is wonderful—she's a lawyer," at cocktail parties, but it's something else to alter radically a lifestyle that included a full-time superwife, i.e., cook, hostess, mother, chauffeur, etc. The strain on the entire family was apparent; the changes produced constant tension between home and work. Life in a "two-man" firm is exceedingly demanding—personally and psychologically: I felt myself diminishing my previous total concentration on the home and domestic life. And yet I felt guilty about neglecting or not performing various household tasks. It seemed to me as if someone was always in tears when I eventually came home. The demands of so small an office, often with no one to turn to for help, wore me out physically and emotionally. I knew that somehow I had to moderate these demands.

Ultimately, we all concluded that I needed to work in a bigger organization where a larger professional staff would allow more flexibility in scheduling.

I decided, as had many other women over the years, to look at government. The federal government had opened up to women lawyers somewhat earlier than other institutions; and there was still a perception that the more ambitious male superstars went into private practice. I went to work at the Federal Trade Commission, an agency where women lawyers were rare. I remained for six years in a variety of positions, ultimately serving as acting director of the Bureau of Consumer Protection. The work was challenging, and it offered visibility and the opportunity to gain a broad spectrum of professional contacts. In short, I flourished and my reputation was enhanced.

I loved the congenial atmosphere fostered by a fresh, innovative new administration [the Carter Administration] committed to reviewing an old agency. The young people there were bright, energetic, and interested in developing new ideas. I was by then more experienced than most, having completed an intense apprenticeship with my brilliant taskmaster classmate, and that training served me well. It was also the beginning of the 1970's, and consumerism, environmentalism, feminism, and other isms were top priorities. I couldn't have felt more at home. But, I had to travel for the first time, and after several months of midnights-filling-the-freezer-with-dinners, I concluded that my family needed liberating, too. They began gradually to take part in household management. They also learned to cook. It was a time for growth for all of us.

The following years in government in politically appointed jobs—as general counsel of the Environmental Protection Agency, and subsequently, of the Department of Health and Human Services—were exciting, stimulating, and demanding. Prior to the Carter years, very few women had ever had the chance to serve in these desirable general counsel jobs. They have been for many years, and still are, considered the most prestigious of legal jobs, often leading to higher office, to the bench, or to partnerships in law firms. The Carter Administration was committed to recruiting qualified women in government. Some of the top men, cabinet officers or agency heads, many of them lawyers, somehow felt more capable of evaluating the credentials of lawyers and, probably more comfortable with them than with other professionals, they filled their "quota" by selecting women general counsels. I clearly benefitted from that search. Almost no one had acquired women through the "old boy" network and, therefore, they reached out to other groups for recommendations of experienced, qualified female lawyers. I was recommended for my first general counsel position by persons I had worked with while at the Federal Trade Commission.

I felt as if I had worked for years to be prepared to do these jobs. My years of practice both in and out of government gave me a base of confidence that I would be able to provide solid but practical advice, plus a mature perspective gained from my years as a housewife, mother, political volunteer, and community worker.

Yet there is no doubt that the arrival of women general counsels at the Departments of Transportation, Defense, and Justice, and at the Environmental Protection Agency, produced, at the least, skepticism. The skills required for success (rather than simple survival) were more than legal: the general counsel always has a chance at being effective and influential. But to really be a major player requires subtle combinations of advocacy and negotiating skills, plus a strong dose of street smarts, usually developed in places where most women had not been admitted. So many expected us to survive but not rise. Nevertheless, many did. For the first time in history, women had the same chances from which generations of male lawyers had benefitted. I am proud to have served a President who contributed uniquely to the status of all women in the United States.

When the inevitable—choosing again a new direction to pursue—was upon me after the 1980 election, it was not surprising that I concentrated on big firms or that, because of my government career,

I had the chance to consider them. The years in government demonstrated that my lifestyle and workstyle were much more compatible with a larger organization. Large firms can offer support advantages —professional and administrative—that small firms can't provide. In addition, I had by then become a specialist in administrative law, and I found that opportunities to practice in a specialty were better with a large firm, where I would have the depth that a federal practice requires as well as the collegial exchange I know I must have.

Although a number of opportunities were available, my choice of Wald, Harkrader & Ross was mostly personal. Practicing with first-rate professionals is essential; finding them in a firm heavily populated by law school classmates and close friends of many years was icing on the cake. Because I knew so many of them, I knew everyone's views in regard to women generally, and women lawyers in particular. The firm had an unusual track record—a woman had been a partner there long before it was fashionable, three women were presently partners at the firm, and the number of women associates ran about 50 percent.

The transition and adjustment to a large firm partnership were much easier than I had anticipated. The concrete barriers of the 1950's were gone—nobody would dream of saying "we don't hire women lawyers." As to gloves, lunch, and other "for women only rules," the young people today shriek with laughter when they hear of such anachronisms. Democratic, progressive, and less stratified than comparable big firms, Wald, Harkrader & Ross has clearly surmounted the tangible barriers of the past.

For me, it is wonderfully refreshing. I am no longer alone. Although I was unaware of missing it, as I now experience the great pleasure of women colleagues, I know why men seemed to have such a good time. The collegiality fostered by the comradeship of being with people—men and women—and of interacting with them on your level is a central part of working together. Indeed, at Wald, Harkrader & Ross, it's all so natural that the women lawyers don't have to defend the fact that they are not best friends with every other woman. There is still pressure to "fit in" as is true wherever we are, but the categories are broader and the possibilities greater. And, again, our numbers, instead of being the "first" or the "only," provide the critical mass I am convinced is necessary for ultimate equality of opportunity.

Still, it's too early to predict even at one law firm how it will all shake out. At the moment, I'm one of three women partners among 40 men partners, but there are 21 women associates compared to 24 men associates. In the past few years, we had more women associates than men. The attrition rate for women, however, is significantly higher, which reduces the number of women who become eligible for partnership. Nevertheless, in the next couple of years, in this and other law firms, a number of outstanding women will be considered for partnership.

Does all this good news mean the legal world is free of sexism? Undoubtedly not. In the 1980's, more subtle, intangible evidence still appears to exist. With more women than ever in more fields everywhere, one sees and hears constant debate as to whether fundamental changes in the control of our society will really happen. For example, after much integration in the military, an announcement was made that many Army jobs will be reclassified "for men only." One suspects that as masses of women move closer to being really "in charge," men's fear of loss of power begins to push them back again. Similarly, when times get tough and jobs get scarcer, those last in tend to be early targets for moving out.

Subtle cultural expressions less obvious than reclassification still haunt the career woman. One recent study described some of these barriers and called one the myth of the "good woman": Society assigns sex rules, and females, from childhood, are somehow expected to be "good," that is, to behave and be morally superior. Most of us believe this at some level. The flip side of the "good woman" is, of course, that we're too good, or too soft, or not tough enough to do tough-minded jobs, or at least not to do them alone. The result of this two-headed myth is that we become anxious and depressed when we think we're not being "good enough." Many women have confirmed to me a feeling of being caught in society's sex-based myths, such as this one.

Such myths are barriers that keep women from full and equal opportunity and from participation in professions such as the law. Another example is that women are seen as powerless, or unable to exercise power as men do for success. Increasingly, when younger women try, they are seen as masculine, cold, humorless, and overly assertive. As a young woman said to me with exasperation, "It's either not enough, or too much. I bought this three-piece suit and I'm called a 'ball-breaker.' What's a person to do?" Still today, as young women lawyers try to "fit in," they must please supervisors by following conventional women's roles, yet demonstrate as well "macho" characteristics traditionally attributed to men.

My view in trying to sort this all out, one which I'm still developing after 30 years, is that, as we struggled so ardently to take our place, we may have confused personal power with strategic power. As Martina Horner, president of Radcliffe College said, "strategic power is more rational and less emotional—construing a strategy to reach your goal has more to do with recognizing that the people you're dealing with don't know how to cope with you, that your presence and position are challenging some of their basic expectations of you *and* of themselves—than what clothes you wear, how aggressively and emotionally you act."

What's in the future? There's good news and bad.

The enormous influx of women lawyers today—an outgrowth of both the women's movement and the Vietnam peace era of the 1960's when activists felt that if they wanted to affect social issues, wanted to change the world, they should become lawyers—creates a viable, critical mass within the business world. The numbers alone considerably ease the threat of subtle barriers. Each of us individually, however, must maintain a constant vigil to see to it that her women colleagues are not subjected to different standards of professional performance or personal demeanor. Many men would probably still prefer "Stepford Wives," at least in the office—ladies who are there to take orders, write perfect memos, and smile a lot. So if a woman is not made from that mold, she may attract more vaguely critical comments than do her male counterparts. With raised consciousness, women will probably recognize and deal with these undercurrents, using their usual skills of intelligence, sensitivity and, I hope, humor.

The bad news is that when the economy lags, it is the women's jobs which suffer from the cutbacks. When faced with this future, things will be tougher for all of us, but especially for women.

CHAPTER 3

AS WASHINGTON LAWYER:
Using Government Experience in Private Practice

BY NANCY L. BUC

Julie Wiatt

NANCY L. BUC

NANCY L. BUC

Weil, Gotshal & Manges
Washington, D.C.

Education

LL.B., University of Virginia School of Law, 1969
A.B., Brown University, 1965 (American civilization)

Experience

Partner, Weil, Gotshal & Manges, 1981-present

Chief Counsel, Food and Drug Administration, 1980-1981, Received Secretary's Special Citation and FDA Award of Merit (January 1981)

Partner, Weil Gotshal & Manges, 1977-1980

Associate, Weil, Gotshal & Manges, 1972-1977

Assistant Director, Bureau of Consumer Protection, Federal Trade Commission, 1972, Received FTC Award for Distinguished Service (October 1972)

Attorney-Advisor to Chairman Miles W. Kirkpatrick, Federal Trade Commission, March 1971-March 1972

Attorney, Federal Trade Commission (Division of Consumer Credit, Division of National Advertising), August 1969-February 1971

Professional Activities

Admitted to practice in District of Columbia, 1978; *in New York,* 1977; *in Virginia,* 1969

Member, Editorial board, *Food, Drug & Cosmetic Law Journal* and *Journal of Products Liability,* 1981-present

Lecturer on FDA, FTC, and Consumer Product Safety Commission topics

Member, American Bar Association (Antitrust Section, 1970-present, chairman of the consumer protection subcommittee of the FTC committee, 1983-present; Administrative Law Section, 1975-present; Corporate, Banking and Business Law Section, 1980-present, co-chairman of the committee on government lawyers, 1981-present)

Member, New York State Bar Association; Association of the Bar of the City of New York, 1977-present

Trustee, Brown University, 1973-1978

Fellow, Brown University, 1980-present (chairman, legal and government affairs committee; member, executive committee)

Personal

Born: July 27, 1944, Orange, N.J.

Single

Chapter 3

AS WASHINGTON LAWYER: USING GOVERNMENT EXPERIENCE IN PRIVATE PRACTICE

BY NANCY L. BUC

On the surface, my resume and my career history look very much like those of many 39-year-old partners in major law firms. Begin in the government. Switch to private practice. Make partner. Take on new responsibilities in opening Washington branch office. Go back into government, this time at senior level. Return to firm, with more responsibility.

A standard high performance career, with the usual awards, trusteeships, etc. But there has been, of course, one major difference: almost everywhere, I was the first woman. First woman to work in the Division of Consumer Credit at the Federal Trade Commission. First woman attorney-adviser to an FTC Chairman. First woman assistant bureau director at the FTC. First woman partner at Weil, Gotshal & Manges. First woman chief counsel at the Food and Drug Administration. Often the first woman lawyer a colleague, an adversary, or a client had ever worked with or against.

When I started law school, the term "woman lawyer" was an oxymoron. Perhaps especially at the University of Virginia, that very Southern, very gentlemanly place (and remembering that the time was 1966, before the Vietnam war and two more assassinations so thoroughly transmuted the fifties into the seventies), the complex of values that meant "woman" was—or was thought to be—inherently and permanently different from the complex of values that meant "lawyer."

Even now, after so many years, I have such sharp memories of that first year in law school. My class of 250, the Class of 1969, had eight women, a quantum leap from the previous high of three. One woman dropped out in our first year. It was much remarked upon as proof that women didn't really want to be lawyers. (To this day, I don't know how many men dropped out. There must have been some, but no one generalized from the individuals to the class.) The remaining seven of us all graduated in the top half of our class—three on Law Review, one on the Moot Court Board.[1] We must have been fairly carefully selected for admission; statistically three or four of us should have been in the bottom half.

That first year was exhilarating and awful. I loved law school, loved working the tight little problems, loved the combination of ancient principles and modern imperatives. I hated the constant harassment: Why are you here? Why would a woman want to be a lawyer? How could a woman be a good lawyer? And, potentially more devastating, the obverse of that last question: If you do turn out to be a good (read aggressive, tough, determined) lawyer, then what kind of woman are you?

Our fellow law students were much tougher on us than the faculty. Perhaps the faculty's greater age, or distinction, or self-confidence, kept them from feeling as threatened as the students seemed to.

One faculty member (let him remain nameless; it doesn't matter any more) used the word "gentlemen" 20 or 30 times an hour. "Now, gentlemen, what is the holding in that case?" "For tomorrow, gentlemen, please read . . . " It seems such a small thing now, but it wasn't then, for it was a thrice weekly reinforcement of what we feared: that women didn't belong, that we would have it tougher, that we weren't wanted. Did he mean it that way? Maybe not, that was just the way he talked, but maybe yes, the way he talked reflected the way he felt. Gentle*men* practiced law, not gentlewomen.

---

1. I was the one on the Moot Court Board. I was denied a place on the National Moot Court team because the team had to travel, the men had traditionally shared hotel rooms, and no one was willing to work out the complicated logistical problems a woman would create. It did not occur to me to protest.

That was the first time, the first of many, many times, that the language issue seemed important to the women but unimportant to the men. Why did they matter so much—these terms like "gentlemen," "lawyers and their wives," "a 40-man firm," "Mr. Justice," and "my brother at the bar?" They mattered because so long as lawyers, especially good lawyers, were thought of as male, I couldn't be one, or at least it would be harder for me to be one. I could be part of a generic group (law student, GS-11 federal government employee, partner), but I could never be part of the fabric of the profession in the way men—whose dominance in the language measured their dominance of the profession—always were assumed to be. I wanted to be part of the fabric of the profession. I wanted to be accepted.

Being accepted was even harder for me, because I was the one who talked. Everyone who has ever known me knows that I talk, that I learn by talking and listening as much as by reading. But women hadn't talked at Virginia unless called upon. I—the combative one who loved the cut and thrust of classroom (and later courtroom) sparring—talked, but I paid a price. Women weren't supposed to talk. I didn't know until years later that many of my female colleagues and some of my male colleagues privately were pleased I had broken the barrier. At the time, I felt isolated and punished.[2]

At the end of my first year, I considered quitting. It all just hurt too much. I didn't quit because I wouldn't give them the satisfaction.

Second year was better.

Third year was better still. Third year brought with it, however, the problem of jobs. I wasn't really aware of the whole process. I didn't know, and no one told me, that all good law students aspired to jobs with Wall Street firms, which had just raised the going rate to $15,000. I had a few interviews (the recruiter from an Orlando firm told me that women didn't litigate in Florida), and the best one was with an FTC lawyer. The Commission made me an offer, and I accepted on the day before Ralph Nader's Raiders issued their

2. I also didn't know until years later that law students are traditionally conflicted about students (male or female) who talk in class. Chalk that lack of knowledge up to another common phenomenon that in 1966 had barely been described: women weren't in the networks, and often had no mentors to teach them the ropes.

report blasting the FTC as incompetent. Surprisingly, that turned out to be a lucky break, for shortly after I arrived at the Commission, things there began to change. First Caspar W. Weinberger, then Miles W. Kirkpatrick, began the task of reviving the agency. I was extremely fortunate to be there while they were doing it.

Before I could do anything useful, however, I had to overcome the usual obstacles. My first boss told me that I shouldn't work nights or weekends because the neighborhood was unsafe and he didn't want me to get hurt. I thanked him for the sentiment, but told him I wanted to be as good as or better than the other GS-11's, and to do that I had to work hard. He relented, and "let" me work nights and weekends.

After a year, I moved to the Advertising Division, and found a case, a co-counsel, and two adversaries who made all the difference in my career. The case was *Topper,* which dealt with false advertising of toy racing car sets and dolls. Topper was represented by Ira M. Millstein and Irving Scher, of whom more later. My co-counsel was Jodie Bernstein, who had just joined the FTC, arriving in a state we would now call a resumed career. She had been away from the practice of law for quite some time to raise a family, and returned to work only to find herself looking at the toy commercials and playing with the toys she claimed to have gone to work to get away from.

What a difference she made to me! For one thing, we became close friends almost immediately. For another, I finally had a female role model, my first. (It was to be over 10 more years before Patricia Roberts Harris became my second.) Jodie was—and is—smart, tough, resourceful, determined, and funny. All the things I wanted to be.*

Jodie and I did well enough with the case that the Commissioners commended us for our work, and the case itself became a landmark in the law of advertising to children.

After that, I went across the street to become attorney-adviser to Chairman Miles W. Kirkpatrick, and once again my life changed for the better. Miles (I called him "sir" at the time) had come to the FTC

**Editor's note: Joan Z. Bernstein's chapter describing her experiences as a lawyer begins on page 31.*

from a traditional Philadelphia firm. I doubt he had ever seen a woman lawyer, much less worked with one. But he accepted me (and Jodie, who worked with us on the 1971 Hearings on Modern Advertising Practice) as part of his Commission family as if it were the most natural thing in the world. He didn't seem to notice that I was different (except that I had pictures of Howdy Doody on my office walls, and was noisier and put more jokes in his speeches than his other assistants). I will never know how he came to this state of grace as far as women lawyers are concerned, but he had, and for nearly two years he taught me how to be a lawyer and protected me from a lot of slings and arrows.

But even he couldn't spare me all of them. Although I was expert in advertising law, a midwestern advertising club refused to allow me to deliver a speech I had written for Miles when he couldn't make it. No women, they said.

Then came Weil, Gotshal & Manges. Ira Millstein, my quondam adversary in *Topper,* called one day in August, 1972, and asked me in his inimitably sarcastic way if I would do him the honor of going to New York to meet people at the firm. I had had no thought of private practice, but I said yes, and by the time I flew home I knew I was headed for New York. (Millstein was startled to discover that I had been promoted so fast at the FTC and that he had to pay me $2,000 a year more than other people in my class at WGM.)

I was still so ignorant of big firms that I didn't know to ask any of the questions about how women were treated.[3] I knew from *Topper* that Millstein and Scher were terrific lawyers, and I knew I could learn from them, and I knew Chairman Kirkpatrick and Ira were fond of each other. That seemed like reason enough.

From the cocoon of the FTC to Weil, Gotshal was quite a transition. Time after time, clients and sometimes WGM partners (and associates) expressed doubt about, or even hostility to, working with a woman. Time after time, Ira or Irv would explain that I was an expert in whatever was needed (generally FTC or Consumer Product Safety Commission work during that period), and I would be thrown

---

3. One partner who interviewed me asked about plans for marriage and children. I told him quite seriously, without questioning the propriety of the inquiry, that I had enough sense not have a baby during the trial of an antitrust case.

in. To this day, I have soft spots in my heart for the clients and colleagues who greeted me warmly or at least accepted me in those early days in private practice when I was new, scared, and rough, especially for Ira and Irv, who went to bat for me over and over just so I could do the work.

And work there certainly was. My problems as a woman lawyer, real as they were and are, fade by comparison to the excellent opportunities I was given at Weil, Gotshal to do work I loved, and which I turned out to be good at.

Weil, Gotshal didn't—and doesn't—discriminate against anybody in handing out work. Especially if you were smart and fast and worked hard, you could do all the challenging, exciting, interesting work you wanted, so I did. I worked for Matsushita Electric Corporation of America (an FDA-mandated recall of television sets, an FTC false advertising case, and a reverse Freedom of Information Act case that twice reached the Supreme Court), Leviton Manufacturing Co. (a CPSC investigation leading to an imminent hazard case in Federal court), Macy's (a CPSC Tris case), Kenyon & Eckhardt (advertising counseling), and many more.

In the process, I learned things big and small—how to write what Irv Scher, who taught me, always called "a Weil, Gotshal product"; how to do subpoena returns (all partners know you do it by reading all the documents; all associates have to learn that by doing it, invariably on hot summer days when the air conditioning is off); how to work with clients; how to dress like a New York lawyer (much easier for men to learn, since they can wear a uniform); how to work with secretaries (in the early 1970's, secretaries were often suspicious of women lawyers; by the late 1970's they often formed a heartwarming part of our support system); and how to stand up in court.

Most important of all, I learned from Ira Millstein how to "do the necessary." "Doing the necessary" can mean fixing the footnotes, but when Ira does it, or asks you to do it, it more usually means "think up some plan, develop some idea, make some move, contact some intermediary, put together some coalition, gin up some study, call some government official, meet with some economist, figure out something—*anything*—to do that will improve your client's position. Then do it."

"Doing the necessary" knows no gender, and I learned to do it well, I think, well enough so that on February 1, 1977, I became my firm's first woman partner.

Not long thereafter, the firm decided that WGM should have a larger presence in Washington, D.C., and I was elected to move to D.C. It made sense, for my practice had become increasingly Washington-oriented, and I was excited about the opportunity to build a Washington practice in the context of a large New York-based firm. It didn't dawn on me until later that few Washington branch offices were headed by people so young, and only one other was headed by a woman. That it didn't dawn on—or matter to—my partners either is a tribute to how far we had all come.

Those early years in Washington—which were also my first few years as a partner—had ups and downs. The Taylor Wine Company was a big up. Taylor had done a comparative taste test in which its new Taylor California Cellars wines had beaten competing wines from Inglenook, Almaden, and Sebastiani, and Taylor wanted to say so in advertising. The Bureau of Alcohol, Tobacco and Firearms said no, even though the proposed ads were truthful in every respect. Taylor's management decided to fight and Mike Doyle, the company's general counsel, and I spent much of 1978 meeting with or suing BATF. We were finally successful in persuading BATF not to take any regulatory action, and had the satisfaction of helping bring to market with effective advertising the key brand of what is now a leading firm in the wine industry.[4]

Equally satisfying, gender played no role at all. Mike Doyle and his colleagues at Taylor seemed only to care whether I had good ideas and could get the job done.

I would not have guessed that it would matter to me when Jimmy Carter came down from his Camp David mountain and fired Joseph A. Califano, Jr., as Secretary of the Department of Health and Human Services, but it did. President Carter replaced Califano with

4. This rather laconic description does not do justice to the excitement of having a client which goes ahead and runs advertising which it believes is true but which could result in criminal penalties or loss of its license to sell wine if BATF disagrees.

Patricia Roberts Harris, who asked Jodie Bernstein to be her General Counsel, who asked me to be Chief Counsel of the Food and Drug Administration.[5]

Working with Jodie again, after a period of eight years, was predictably a pleasure. The opportunity to work with Mrs. Harris was a bonus. I had read about her in the newspapers in 1965, when Lyndon Johnson named her Ambassador to Luxembourg, again in 1969 when she was briefly Dean of the Howard Law School, and of course when she was appointed Secretary of The Department of Housing and Urban Development, and I had met her when Brown University, of which I was a trustee, awarded her an honorary degree in 1972. Nothing had prepared me for the sheer presence and force of this woman, nor for the sharpness and excellence of her mind, nor for the excitement of working with her. When she wanted something, she wanted it now, and she wanted it right. In return, she gave it her full attention, and you got the satisfaction of knowing that your work had been understood.

My high regard for her was not universal, however. Many at FDA preferred that the agency be more independent of the department than Secretary Harris would allow, and were reluctant to be as responsive to her and the departmental apparatus as she wished. I remember vividly one meeting at which she rather forcefully expressed her unhappiness about FDA's handling of a drug policy issue, and many FDA staff were openly defiant about her right to set policy for FDA. I thought then and remain convinced that these men (they were virtually all men at FDA; not only was I the first female general counsel of the agency, I was the only female senior staff member and one of a handful of women in policy positions of any kind) would not have dared to so express themselves to a male Secretary.

Indeed, qualities that are so often counted virtues in men—toughness, brilliance, being a demanding boss—were thought by many (men) to be defects in Pat Harris. She has had to put up with that for years, and has triumphed over it. I loved watching her do it even as I hated knowing that she had to.

5. FDA is a component agency of The Department of Health and Human Services, and the FDA Chief Counsel is also an Assistant General Counsel of HHS.

Almost everyone who has ever held policy-level government positions would give the same answer to the question of why we would give up high salaries and much of our privacy:[6] the problems one gets to work on in the government are wonderfully complex, significant, and interesting. My term at FDA included contentious Congressional hearings on infant formula, on the drug DMSO, and on contact lenses; an agency decision to continue the ban on cyclamates; rulemaking on nitrites and caffeine; and regulation of tampons in connection with toxic shock syndrome. With issues like that to work on, I would have paid them!

Two days after President Carter lost the election, I had dinner with Ira Millstein to tell him I wanted to return to Weil, Gotshal, which I did on January 21, 1981, the day after President Reagan was inaugurated.[7]

Since 1981, WGM's Washington office has doubled in size, and we're working on an exceptionally diverse array of problems. On many days, the issue of being a woman lawyer never comes up. Often, though, it does—a client or prospective client who's still dubious (rarely actually hostile, these days) about women lawyers; questions from law students about WGM's treatment of women (it's excellent, but there are still, as there are everywhere, occasional day-to-day problems and misunderstandings); someone (as often as not an ally) whom you're trying to persuade but who just can't seem to hear what you're saying.

All in all, I've been lucky to be a part of a great firm, to be able to make some contribution in government, and to have Bernsteins, Kirkpatricks, Millsteins, and Harrises to teach me and become my friends. But it would have been OK, too, if it had been a little easier.

---

6. The issue of *Legal Times* which contained my partnership income from the year before I went to FDA was closely scrutinized by FDA lawyers and the amount was quickly reported to other FDA people.

7. Those last months of the Carter Administration told us a lot about the status of women. I was lucky enough to have a law firm to come home to, but many of my female colleagues—bright, energetic women who had held high government positions—found it difficult to get jobs commensurate with their ability and experience. One four-year cycle of women-in-high-positions-in-government had not had as much effect on people's heads as we had hoped.

CHAPTER 4

AS PARTNER IN A SMALL FIRM: Setting the Stage for Maternity Leave

BY MARNA S. TUCKER

Ann Zelle

MARNA S. TUCKER

MARNA S. TUCKER

Boasberg, Klores, Feldesman & Tucker
Washington, D.C.

Education

LL.B., Georgetown Law Center, 1965; Board of Editors, *Georgetown Law Journal*

B.S., University of Texas, 1962 (education and government)

Experience

Partner, Boasberg, Klores, Feldesman & Tucker, 1973-present

Director, Project to Assist Interested Law Firms in Pro Bono Publico Programs, 1971-1973; Section of Individual Rights and Responsibilities, American Bar Association

Special Assistant to Congressman Allard K. Lowenstein, 1969-1970

Deputy Director, Legal Services Program, Office of Economic Opportunity, San Francisco, Calif., 1967-1969

Staff Attorney, Neighborhood Legal Services Project, Washington, D.C., 1965-1967

Professional Activities

Admitted to practice in District of Columbia, 1966; *in California,* 1969

President-elect, District of Columbia Bar, 1983-1984

American Bar Association: Chairperson of Section of Individual Rights and Responsibilities 1982-1983; Chairman, Commission on Public Understanding about the Law, 1979-1982; Member of the House of Delegates, 1974-1980; Fellow, American Bar Foundation; Officer of Section of Individual Rights and Responsibilities, 1977-1981; President's Advisory Committee, 1978-1979; Member of Council of Section of Individual Rights and Responsibilities, 1975-1977; Special Committee on Public Interest Practice, 1973-1979

District of Columbia Bar (Unified): President-elect, 1983; Member of the Board on Professional Responsibility (Disciplinary Board), appointed 1977-1983 by D.C. Court of Appeals; Steering Committee of Division on Courts, Lawyers, and

Administration of Justice, 1974-1977; Member of Ethics Committee, 1974-1976; Chairperson, *Pro Bono Symposium* Committee, 1975; Bar Delegate to ABA House of Delegates, 1974-1980

United States Circuit Court Committee on Admissions and Grievances, 1979-present

United States Judicial Nominating Commission for the District of Columbia, 1977-1980; appointed by President Jimmy Carter

Center for Law and Social Policy, Board of Trustees, 1977-present

National Women's Law Center, Board of Trustees, 1981-present

National Legal Aid and Defender Association, Vice-President, 1972-1977

National Lawyers Committee for Civil Rights Under Law, Executive Committee, 1973-present

Washington Lawyers Committee for Civil Rights Under Law, Executive Committee, 1973-present

ACLU of the National Capital Area, Board of Directors, 1973-1976

Adjunct Professor of Law, Georgetown University Law Center, 1972

Lecturer of Law, Catholic University, Columbus School of Law, 1972-1974

Lecturer, Poverty Law and Legislation for Reginald Heber Smith Fellowship Attorney Training Program (University of Southern California), 1970

Publications

"The Judge's Role in Educating the Public About the Law" 31 *Catholic University Law Review* 201 (1982)

Nader and Green, *Verdicts on Lawyers,* Chapter on "Pro Bono ABA" Thomas Y. Crowell Co., 1976

Access to Justice in the United States: The Economic Barriers and Some Promising Solutions, University of Southern California, Social Science Research Institute, 1976 (one of several authors)

Rape and Its Victims: A Report for Citizens, Health Facilities, and Criminal Justice Agencies, published by the National Institute of Law Enforcement and Criminal Justice, November 1975

Pro Bono Publico or Pro Bono Organized Bar? 60 *American Bar Association Journal* 916 (1974)

The Lawyer As a Volunteer: Pro Bono Publico Programs for Bar Association

and Professional Organizations, published by American Bar Association, 1972

"The Private Lawyer and Public Responsibility—The Profession's Armageddon," 51 *Nebraska Law Review* 367 (1972)

"Pro Bono Publico" 30 *N.L.A.D.A. Briefcase 13* (September 1971)

The Private Law Firm and Pro Bono Publico Programs: A Responsive Merger, published by ABA, 1972

"Legislative Advocacy and Law Reform" — *Materials for Reginald Heber Smith Fellowship Attorney Training Program,* published by Western Center for Law and Poverty, October, 1970

"Justice in Sneakers: A Neighborhood Law Office in Operation;" Distribution by OEO, 1966, cited in *Harvard Law Review,* February, 1967

Personal

Born: March 5, 1941, Philadelphia, Penn.
Married: 1973
Children: Two, born in 1975 and 1980.

Chapter 4

AS PARTNER IN A SMALL FIRM: SETTING THE STAGE FOR MATERNITY LEAVE

BY MARNA S. TUCKER

It's the end of one more day that seemed to fly by without my breaking stride in a hectic schedule. Tonight I want to write this article. I want to share my experiences as a woman lawyer in a small firm with others who may be treading the same path. I hope that by reading about my experiences, they won't feel as isolated as I did, will see the humor where I did not, and will know that their own contradictory feelings of insecurity and fulfillment are probably normal and healthy ones.

But I'd also like to play my guitar tonight, do some pastel drawings like I did in high school, and wake up my baby to snuggle my nose into his warm little neck. Probably, only the article will get written, because I've made it my priority for the evening. It's simply one more trade-off in a life full of trade-offs.

It's because of my heavy schedule, and my life of trade-offs that I think I'm probably typical of women lawyers in the 1980's. There aren't a whole lot of us. We haven't been around long enough for people to do major studies about our lives, our stresses and strains, the side-effects on our families. And even if these studies did exist, I wouldn't have the time to read them.

Perhaps a few vital facts about myself would provide an appropriate backdrop to sharing the experiences I have had as a woman partner in a small law firm: I am slightly over 40, went to law school immediately upon graduation from college, and was graduated from law school in the mid-1960's, when the Civil Rights Movement was at its peak and the anti-Vietnam era was just beginning. I married at age 32 (considered then to be "terribly late"), which was a great relief to my mother (and to me!). I have two young children: the youngest was born when I was 40, which has had the effect of delaying, if not avoiding, a midlife crisis. I am happily married to the same man—also a lawyer. Of our friends, most of whom are lawyer couples who practice fast-paced law in Washington, D.C., we are in the small minority of happily marrieds. Most of our friends are either divorced or appear to be on the verge of it.

I feel good about my career, my marriage, my children, and myself. Right now, it's all hanging together well. I don't feel driven to achieve some excessively laudatory goal. I don't feel any unexplained emptiness or tension inside. I look forward to waking up every day. Sure, I want some things I don't have. But somewhere along the way—I don't know when—I accepted the fact that I couldn't do or have it all. Once that happened, everything was easier.

Why did I choose to practice in a small law firm? To answer that, I must go back to my law school graduation, when career choices were extremely limited because of overt bias against women lawyers. I knew then it was unrealistic to think I'd become a partner in a major Washington law firm. So I didn't try. The relatively few women lawyers in Washington in the mid-1960's chose government careers, became public defenders, or did estate and probate work in small firms.

It was a time of idealism, so as the federally-sponsored anti-poverty program was just getting started, I chose to join one of the first legal services programs for the poor. I felt then that I was doing important work and improving the world. I made a good salary, I got to litigate, and I had my own clients right away.

Over the next few years, I moved to positions of greater responsibility in the federal government. I traveled to nice places, went to scores of meetings, met interesting people, and made an even better income, but was never really challenged as a lawyer. Deep down, I felt it was all too easy. The real test of a lawyer's mettle had to be in private practice. Would people actually pay me money to represent them? For six years, the doubts I had about succeeding in private practice propelled me from one interesting short-term government job to the next. But the gnawing I felt inside finally became so great that I started to make timid inquiries among small firms.

It never occurred to me to inquire at a large firm. A "lateral entry" was a rarity then and I had no specialty and no clients to offer. In Washington, mid-level government lawyers were (and still are) in abundance. Those things, on top of being a woman, limited my options severely. A small firm was appealing to me because I have always been more comfortable in smaller settings than in large groups. In addition, I thought that being a big fish in a small pond would make it easier to balance the demands of family and career.

So I joined a small law firm as a partner with seven men. The firm was about a year old and was not exactly flush. Starting as a partner had little significance monetarily because getting a piece of the profits is no big deal when there are few to share. But joining the firm had great emotional significance to me because those seven men had decided that I could share their professional destiny on an equal basis. I was about eight years younger than any of them—and I was the only woman.

Being the only woman is a love-hate thing for me. I hate it because I feel so alone about certain things that men cannot understand: how it feels to be ignored by a maitre d' in a restaurant when you've got an important client; how it feels to knock yourself out on a problem and the only comment is "You've got beautiful brown eyes"; and how it feels to be three months pregnant, exhausted, and have nobody know why you are cranky. But I also love being special and having someone say "How do you do it all?"

Because I was the only woman, I felt enormous pressure to prove myself to my partners by bringing in business. I felt that they had taken a gamble to hire me. (It never occurred to me that I might have taken the gamble by choosing them.) But at first I had no clients, so I took what my partners doled out to me. I was really much more of an "associate" than a partner in my functions, and I worked hard to do the best legal job for them that I could.

Initially, relationships in the firm worked rather easily because I took this subservient position. I did my partners' work and reported to them. I wasn't a threat; I was playing a typical dependent woman's role.

But as time passed, the dynamics changed. Because I did all the less glamorous work, I developed a store of information that no one else had. My partners had to ask me about more and more. For example, I was the partner sent down to court to argue unimportant motions. Pretty soon, I was the one who knew the judges, the clerks, and where to stand in the courtroom. Furthermore, because going to court and putting it all on the line is a scary proposition for anyone, my partners relinquished responsibility for more important cases as well. Soon I had two feathers in my bonnet—I had information, and I could go to court. My partners started to need me. That was when life started getting difficult.

Although I never felt I was in competition with my partners, I think my being a woman made them unconsciously competitive with me. As I moved from a dependent to a more assertive role in the firm, I became a threat to some of the men. For whatever psychological reasons, some of my partners kept putting me down. I don't want to attribute this solely to my being a woman, but I do feel that the unique competition between the sexes makes it more likely to occur.

The clearest example of how I was treated differently as a woman occurred when I got pregnant. I had been with the firm about a year and a half. We were still not affluent; I had a very small client base. By this time, I had developed some warm and respectful relationships with several of my partners. The issue of how much time I would take off for maternity leave needed to be resolved.

I wanted to take off two months with no reduction in my income, but I felt that my partners thought I'd be sitting at home watching the soaps and eating bonbons for two months. I remember the terrible pressure to come back to work as soon as I could to prove that women can have babies and continue working as if nothing had happened. My later conversations with other women in similar circumstances confirm that this pressure to return immediately is a very common phenomenon. Unfortunately, I allowed those thoughts to mar what should have been an extraordinary time in my life. Childbirth is so special that I wish I hadn't put myself through the last-minute effort of finishing up a client's report. (I sure didn't do it the second time around.)

Some of my partners also believed that since having a baby was a voluntary act, they shouldn't have to financially support my choice to do so. In a small firm, paying two months' salary without having two months of a lawyer's billing is a real financial drain. Maternity leave policies providing up to six months pay are a luxury only large institutions can afford. Some of my partners felt ripped off; we all felt it was a difficult problem. I think they wanted to be fair to me—and fair to themselves.

We finally resolved the dilemma with a lawyerly solution: We agreed that every partner could have a three-month sabbatical with pay every five years to do whatever he or she wanted. My sabbatical would be first. Sounds fair? It was absurd! In a small firm, it is difficult enough to coordinate short vacations. The logistics of three-month stints for every partner on top of regular vacations for the rest are impossible! I got my sabbatical, but none of them ever tried to take theirs, and as long as that state of affairs exists, resentment festers.

The next time the issue of my maternity leave came up, my partners had learned that women lawyers can have babies and then come back and bill their hours. They also learned that I cared about the firm just as much as they did. Most importantly, we all learned that a small partnership is like a marriage. If you are in it for the long haul, you try to accommodate each partner's differences.

Maternity leave in the abstract is one thing. Taking a two-month maternity leave in the context of a long-term partnership is quite another. Now when someone goes on maternity leave, the attitude of the firm is better. We don't apply strict rules; we accommodate. Maternity leave has become a time-management problem, not a matter of principle.

A more difficult maternity-related problem than time off developed when I returned to work. Before the baby came, I'd leave work at about 6:00 p.m. Since I was nursing my baby and needed to go home by 4:00 each day to feed her, I announced to my partners that I would be leaving early every day for the next few months. But I'd be taking work home so that my billable hours would not decline. Besides, I added, I came in earlier than any of my partners.

I was not prepared for the uproar that followed. My partners felt that the hours worked was not the point. They believed that by not being available in the office for 5:00 meetings, informal discussions, and general partnership interchange, I was not fulfilling the obligations of partnership. All my protestations to the contrary, they were immovable and they docked my partnership share for the hours I was not in the office. I still resent that decision, and it sometimes colors my reaction to other partnership matters even now, eight years later. I cannot recall one 5:00 partnership meeting, one informal exchange that could not have occurred at another time, or one day when all partners were even in the office at 5:00. The year I was nursing I billed as many, if not more hours than any of my other partners.

The bitterness I felt during the nursing period was almost enough to make me want to leave the firm. My partners were saying to me, if you want to nurse your baby you have to pay for it, whether or not it costs us anything. I translated that into a lack of respect for me as a lawyer and as a woman.

What sustained me through that period was support and affection from my husband. At that time, he had an important position on the White House staff, with over 600 people working for him. He could have worked until 10:00 every night. But every afternoon at 4:00 he'd leave his office, pick me up, drive me home and read to me while I nursed the baby. What my husband said with those deeds has been a cornerstone in our marriage: his actions told me that he believed my work was as important as his work; that he wanted to be with our child as much as I did and was prepared to make the same professional sacrifices; that men can and do set priorities of family ahead of work; and that he was not embarrassed to let the White House and his staff know what his priorities were.

As my place in the firm became more secure and the personal relationships with my partners strengthened, the partnership learned again that I wasn't ripping them off by leaving early. Over the years, they came to trust my judgment. The question of time in the office never came up when I had my second baby, and it was never mentioned for any other women lawyers who followed.

Another example of how I was treated differently as a woman revolved around what is truly a difficult experience in any law firm—the ousting of a partner. The early years in our firm were so focused on economic survival that we rarely examined the kind of work we were doing, but once we felt that the firm had a solid client base, we began to realize that one of the partners was out of step in his approach to our practice. We spent more and more time caucusing about problems with the errant partner. While no one wanted to confront in the office the possibility of a split, we each complained constantly to our spouses at home.

After several difficult months of increasing tension, we finally met to discuss asking this partner to leave the firm. The male partners, many of whom had been his close personal friends since college, were distraught. They couldn't easily put aside their friendship for the economic and psychological well-being of our firm. In addition, I think they readily identified with a middle-age man with a family to support looking for a new job. I spoke my mind, but was far from being the driving force behind the decision. I couldn't have been even if I wanted to be—the close friends had to do it.

After our partner left the firm, I heard through the grapevine that he blamed me as the "Dragonlady." He said that I had manipulated the entire move because of my ambition to rise in the firm. Frankly, I find it amazing that he could attribute so powerful a role to me. But as the only woman, and the person least interwined in his life, I was the easiest to blame. Being a scapegoat is one of the roles women play in small firms.

After this disruption, the firm faced a new milestone. We had to decide whether to promote one of our women associates to partnership. She had been with the firm for five years and, besides being a terrific lawyer, had earned the respect of us all as a warm and level-headed person. As we debated whether to allow this woman into the inner sanctum of partnership, I recalled the discussion five years earlier when we were deciding whether to hire her as an associate. At that meeting, one of my partners stated that we didn't have to pay her as much as a male associate because she was married and her husband could support their family. He thought he was being truly liberated merely in hiring a woman. I pounced on him! To his credit, he's learned about equal pay.

After this second woman became a partner, we hired two more women associates. By that time, the proportion of men and women in our small firm was about half and half, and the atmosphere had changed dramatically. I wasn't alone anymore. There was always someone I could talk to about how tough it was to fit the nursery school carpool and a 9:15 court appearance into the same morning. There was a silent understanding about what it means to have your babysitter not show up one day without telling you. There were winks across the partnership table when some partner would make an unwitting sexist remark. To have a woman colleague with whom to share the law firm experience actually made it fun. In the business world and the social world alike, men need their boyfriends and women need their girlfriends.

In addition to feeling less alone, I noticed other changes. It was now the norm to have women lawyers around. The men no longer thought it unusual, and neither did I. Once we had the critical mass of women, the dynamics changed for everybody. I no longer felt the pressure to show that I could do everything well simply to prove that I was as serious as the men. The men stopped feeling they had to explain that I was their "female" partner. We all got down to business without being sidetracked by any sexist preoccupations.

The women in my firm (and I include myself) take their profession beyond being just a good lawyer. They, more than the men, have been very active in professional and bar association activities. For example, I decided early in my career that women need to make themselves known through professional activities because most of us don't have the business-getting network of contacts that men acquire through their clubs and male business friends. My theory proved correct for me; through bar association activities I got to know a wide variety of other lawyers. When other lawyers know your name, it helps your professional reputation and confidence even if they do not know what you do, or how well you do it.

As I progressed to more responsible positions in these outside organizations, the time I devoted to them necessarily increased, but at the same time, my responsibility to the law firm engendered an unrelenting pressure to bill hours. I found that my lunch hours disappeared so that I could bill my necessary hours each day, while continuing my professional association activities. I found that after I put the kids to sleep at night, I'd be working on something. I liked the outside activities and the people I met, and I didn't mind juggling my hours. I liked the recognition I was beginning to attain.

My partners, however, while occasionally congratulating me for some appointment or honor, could not have cared less about my outside work. Mostly, they cared about the dollars I brought in, not the honors, although they never expressed displeasure, and they always agreed to my use of our firm support staff for my projects. From conversations I've had with men who have been active in bar association activities, I have learned that this response is not unique to women. Law firms, especially small law firms, are money-making propositions. Any expenditure of time that does not directly lead to expanding the income of the firm is not as important. This attitude, however, can have a greater impact on women because they have to spend more time developing new ways of getting known in the legal marketplace and of getting business other than through the "boys' club" network.

In retrospect, I think I worried too much about bringing in business and billing hours. The pressure was there, but my own self-expectations made it worse. Early in my partnership, one of my male partners, sensing the pressure I was under to bring in a "big client" tried to make me lighten up by telling this story with great affection: When he was a little boy in Brooklyn, there was a candy store on his street corner. In front of the candy store was a peanut machine—the kind that you put a penny in and got four peanuts. He learned that the candy store owner got a piece of the profits from the peanut machine, the peanut company got a piece of the profits, and the mob got a piece of the profits—all from his little contributions. From that he learned the significance of pennies. Hence, his story illustrated the importance of small clients. Had I relaxed a little about the "big one," and given myself some time, I probably would have built my practice at the same rate, but with greater enjoyment.

Belonging to a small firm has the advantage over a large firm of allowing more intimate knowledge and appreciation of your partners and your business. Because I am a part of our decision-making, from secretaries' raises to whether we purchase a building, I have no doubt that the law firm is my law firm. I feel the responsibility, the sharing of burdens with my partners, and the pride.

As a woman, though, I react to the burdens differently. I have always felt that I had a peculiar freedom of choice about working. I chose my career based solely on what I wanted to do; I never believed that I had to be a bread-winner. Deep down, I thought that I didn't have to worry about making money because someone would always take care of me. The facts were to the contrary—I had to work my way through college and law school; I supported myself solely after law school until I married; I contributed equally to my family's support. Yet somewhere in the recesses of my mind, I bought the line that was popular among my girl friends when I was younger—that women only worked because they wanted to work, not because they had to work.

Because I enjoyed this peculiar freedom of thinking that I didn't have to work, I have always spoken my mind and been very straightforward with my partners, without fear of jeopardizing my financial security. I zero in on difficult issues and make decisions with relative ease. But about a year ago, my husband started his own law practice, which meant we would be strained financially for awhile. Our family became almost solely dependent on my income. On top of that, my law firm's records began to show that I was bringing in a substantial portion of the firm's business, and that my partners were more financially dependent upon me than ever before. I felt trapped and depressed. I realized then that I had to work, that my freedom was a myth and always had been. For the first time I knew the pressure of being a breadwinner for my family and my partners—the same pressure that men probably feel all the time. I didn't like it one bit. I wonder how many women who are driving hard for a successful career feel the way I did. And if they do, is it any wonder that men get mixed signals about how serious a woman lawyer is about her career?

Now work is an essential part of my life, financially and intellectually, and like so many other women, I engage in an unrelenting struggle to balance work, children, marriage, and personal needs. In terms of my work, I am no different from a man. But men rarely seem to engage in the struggle I experience. They seldom think about setting priorities among work and family obligations.

This contrast was illustrated a few months ago when I participated in a panel before a group of lawyers on "The Art of Rain-making." I was amazed to be asked to participate on such a topic. I never viewed myself as a "business-getter," certainly not by Washington, D.C. standards, the birthplace of "superlawyers." After our presentations, the panel members were asked how we set our priorities in managing our lives. One, a former Cabinet member, expounded on the need to work, work, work. He said the superlawyers of Washington worked more hours a day and night than the traditional hard-driven young lawyers. If you want to be a superlawyer, his message went, you have to want that more than anything else, and be prepared for hard and unrelenting work, to the sacrifice of family and personal pleasure.

When my turn came, I presented choices that were much different. I didn't want to be a superlawyer. Not at that price. Nor did I want to be a supermom and superwife with overloaded expectations. I knew that was impossible. I would be thrilled with a grade of "B" for a good job as a lawyer and a good job as a wife and mother. It is a very personal thing, setting priorities and acknowledging human limitations. My family is most important to me. My career is only fun when my mind and heart are at ease about family concerns. That's not to say my career is not important. I'm a good mother and wife only because I like what I am separate and apart from those domestic roles. I am a package deal, and the parts are simply not as good as the whole.

I joined a small firm so I could put all these parts together—so I could have the freedom, for example, to walk away from the office and go to my children's swim meet at 11:00 in the morning, without anyone raising an eyebrow. I chose a small firm so I could impress my own values on it, and not simply have the firm impress its values on me. It has taken time to be able to do this. A small law firm is an ever-evolving relationship just as a marriage is. I've chosen good mates in both my firm and my marriage (I think luck had as much to do with that as anything else), but it's a question of more than making the right choices. You have to know what you want and be prepared to juggle demands and time to get it.

Never were my many roles as clear to me as the day I attended a meeting at the White House. The meeting was scheduled for 9:00 a.m. I woke up at 6:30 a.m., put on my super-special pink ultra-suede suit and had a rushed breakfast with the kids and my husband. I piled my daughter into the car because it was my turn to carpool to nursery school. After dropping off the little ones to the tune of "Old MacDonald Had A Farm," I rushed to the White House. Parking nearby was impossible, but I finally managed and ran to the White House out of breath and very excited. I gradually relaxed in the meeting and began to enjoy my powerful surroundings. I remember thinking as I examined the mahogany table and chairrails around the room: "Tucker, you have finally made it! You have reached the pinnacle of your career." Then I looked down at my pink ultra-suede skirt and saw five grape jelly fingerprints neatly emblazoned on my lap.

CHAPTER 5

AS LEGAL SERVICES ATTORNEY: Working for the Community

BY LOIS WOOD

Diane H. Weyermann

LOIS WOOD

LOIS WOOD

Land of Lincoln Legal Assistance Foundation, Inc.
East St. Louis, Ill.

Education

J.D., Harvard Law School, 1974; cum laude

B.A., Michigan State University, 1969; Phi Beta Kappa (political science)

Experience

Directing Attorney, Land of Lincoln Legal Assistance Foundation, Inc., East St. Louis office, 1978-present

Staff Attorney, Land of Lincoln Legal Assistance Foundation, Inc., East St. Louis office, 1974-1978

Student Member, Harvard Legal Aid Bureau, 1972-1974

Professional Activities

Admitted to practice in Illinois, 1974

Member, Board of Directors, St. Clair County (Ill.) Bar Association, 1983-present

Member, Board of Directors, National Social Science & Law Center, 1979-present

Chairperson, Management Advisory Committee, Land of Lincoln Legal Assistance Foundation, Inc., 1981-present

Coordinator, Illinois Housing Task Force, 1983

Chairperson, Housing Committee, Land of Lincoln Legal Assistance, 1978-1981

Member, Legal Services Corporation Advisory Committee, Quality Improvement Project, 1977-1978

Member, Legal Services Corporation Advisory Committee on Turnover, 1977

Member, Study Team, National Consumer Law Center, 1976

Publications

"Opposition to Hospital Closings. The Role of Attorneys in Coalitions,"

Clearinghouse Review, April 1981, Vol. 14, p. 1228 (co-authored with Mulvanny)

"Rights of Purchasers under Installment Contracts for the Sale of Residential Property," a chapter in *Representing Residential Tenants,* Illinois Institute of Continuing Legal Education, 1983

Personal

Born: Jan. 20, 1949, Plainview, Neb.
Married: 1968

Chapter 5

AS LEGAL SERVICES ATTORNEY: WORKING FOR THE COMMUNITY

BY LOIS WOOD

I have been a legal services lawyer in East St. Louis, Ill. for nine years. During that time I have helped people with problems ranging from mortgage foreclosures to domestic violence. I have helped keep a hospital open in a poor community, have assisted clients in changing the arbitrary admissions system of the local housing authority, and have forced the U.S. Department of Housing and Urban Development (HUD) to provide low income housing assistance in the county where I work. I am successful as a legal services attorney not only because I have achieved those results, but because I have succeeded in staying in legal services by choice with continued enthusiasm for my work. I am not alone in such success. There are hundreds of legal services workers throughout the country who have also achieved good results for individual clients, who have had occasional victories that have improved the lives of greater numbers of people, and who still derive satisfaction from practicing law on behalf of those who can not otherwise afford an attorney.

Most people have only the most vague sense of what a legal services attorney does. The week in which I was asked to write this chapter was an interesting one, and it occurred to me that a summary of its highlights would give an idea of what my work and life are like.

I started the weekend on a light note, attending an Illinois State Bar Association sports award breakfast. I was there to accept my trophy for winning the women's division of the five kilometer race at the ISBA annual meeting. I was excited to have won, having only been running for six months. The breakfast was also a good opportunity to talk with private attorneys from throughout the state whose support has been incredibly important to legal services during the past three years.

But the rest of the day was not so pleasant. The board of directors of Land of Lincoln Legal Assistance Foundation, for which I work, had called a special meeting at noon. The subject—the need to reduce our spending in 1983 and 1984 because of the federal cutbacks in legal services funding over the past three years. The news was bad because we had already laid off workers in 1981. Yet the foundation staff—after three days of meetings which I chaired—had prepared a report with recommendations to the board for a new staff reduction plan. I had written up our proposal and was there to present it to the board. Joseph Bartylak, our executive director, accepted our staff reduction plan and asked the board to adopt it. But some board members still hoped that the situation would improve enough by the end of 1983 so that no cutbacks would be necessary; they wanted to defer even planning the cutbacks until then. After a long and heated meeting, the board decided to accept most parts of our plan and to send out layoff notices by July 15th. The meeting was considered successful—but that did not make the result any less painful.

The following Monday, I worked on individual clients' cases for much of the day, and at 4:00 we had our weekly office meeting of attorneys and paralegals. Some weeks our staff meetings are discussions of cases and issues that have arisen during the week. This one was mostly administrative: we discussed the board of directors meeting, client in-take procedures, and some programs to involve private attorneys in the delivery of legal services. One legal issue did come up: a community group asked for our assistance on a project that could mean more jobs for blacks and women in the area. Would it be at all possible for one or more of us to find time to work on it? No decision was reached, although we knew it would have to be made soon.

Tuesday was much the same; I worked my way through some of my individual cases. I also interviewed by phone two new, and rather distraught, clients who had emergencies that just couldn't wait until my next interview opening. One, I was able to resolve with advice over the phone. I scheduled an appointment with the other caller so I could look at her papers before tackling her problem.

A low-income public housing tenants group also called during the day. Would I be available for their next meeting to discuss the legal rights of tenants during a current public housing crisis? They said that HUD was again threatening to take away the housing subsidy to the local housing authority; I agreed to come to their meeting.

The main event on Wednesday was a meeting in our Mt. Vernon, Ill. office to discuss our foundation's private bar involvement program, which is administered out of their office. Because a minority private bar involvement program will soon be administered out of my office, I attended the Mt. Vernon meeting to help work out procedures for both.

First thing Thursday morning I wanted to find out what happened at a court hearing the previous afternoon. Two of our attorneys, Tom Kennedy and Diane Weyermann, represented handicapped children who were told by a school district that they could not return to summer school because of a reduction in state funding. The children are severely retarded and, if their education is abruptly halted, they could lose the skills it has been so difficult for them to learn. The news was good! The judge granted a temporary restraining order requiring the school district to provide education for the remainder of the summer session. A hearing was ordered before fall to determine if the school district will continue services then.

Late Thursday afternoon, I attended my first meeting of the St. Clair County Bar Association board of directors. I am the first woman ever to be elected to the board of directors. The election was important to me because I know that the bar association will be instrumental in determining whether a new *pro bono* program being set up state-wide will have any success in encouraging private attorneys to do free legal work for the poor in our county.

On Friday, Nancy Molland, an attorney in our office, Jack Ver Steegh, the program's litigation coordinator, and I continued discussions regarding settlement of a major lawsuit. A number of black and white clients had sued HUD, the county, the city of Belleville, and a local housing authority in a civil rights action regarding low income housing in Belleville. HUD had earlier committed funds for the construction of public housing. Some community resistance developed, however, apparently out of fear that blacks would move from East St. Louis, which is 96 percent black, to the adjoining community of Belleville, which is 98 percent white. HUD had acquiesced to the resistance and dropped plans to fund the housing. Later, in response to the law suit, HUD offered to restore the funding and use it for rehabilitation of low income housing. Their offer meant that $3 million of housing assistance would be provided to low income people in the county during the next 15 years. We and our clients were tremendously pleased by the offer, and it was a joy to draft so favorable a settlement agreement.

Again, at least part of the day was much less pleasant. I sat down to talk with one of our senior attorneys about current problems in the office. The stresses of the past year and a half are showing here: We have cut back the staff by two attorneys and now only have six available to serve the needs of more than 45,000 poor people in two counties. One more lawyer will be laid off in October. As the resources have dwindled, our problems have increased. There are more poor people than ever before, and, as a result of other federal cutbacks, more of them are in desperate circumstances when they call our office for help. By now tension has developed among the staff over whether the attorney with whom I met was making the best possible use of time. We discussed it for a long time; finally, we resolved to make some changes in work assignments after talking with the rest of the staff.

At last, it is Saturday again. Today I have been home on my farm. A private attorney called with good news: He had just received an opinion reinstating the social security benefits of a disabled client whom he and I both represent. The man was terminated from social security disability benefits during the huge wave of terminations which started in 1981. Since then, he, his wife, and their five children have been surviving on her low salary as a nurse's aide. They have been able to stay in their house only because I have successfully represented him in an effort to forestall foreclosure of his HUD insured mortgage. The successful social security appeal means that the struggle to keep the family in their home for those two years was worthwhile; he will be able to reinstate his mortgage and make payments in the future.

I turned my attention to the farm, which my husband, Jim Hunsley, and I purchased four years ago to begin a pick-your-own berry and vegetable business. Our first crop of blackberries was ripening, and I spent much of the morning calling customers. The rest of the day I worked in our herb garden and orchard. Jim devoted himself to farm work. Late in the evening we finally have a chance to talk. The discussion is about children. Can we afford to have a child? How will we find the time to raise a baby? Do we have enough money to expand or rehabilitate our house to make room for a child? We don't resolve the problem, but we come closer. We cannot wait much longer. I am 34 and Jim is 43.

During the weekend, I also found time to work on this chapter. Because I have been asked to write about myself, I sat in our yard and began thinking about how I got here. I remember the farm in Nebraska where I grew up, never having met a lawyer.

* * *

During the first ten years of my life, I lived on a small farm in rural Nebraska. I am the fourth in a family of nine brothers and sisters. We all assumed our share of the work early, and for me that meant washing dishes, caring for the younger children, and as I grew older, doing more and more of the gardening.

At times my brothers and sisters and I made up almost half the students in the one-room school house a mile from where we lived. I had learned to read from an older sister before starting school and soon skipped a grade. I loved reading and my parents took me to the town library every week for a fresh supply of books. As a result, school came easily to me, and I was never bored since, in the one-room school, I could always listen to the lessons of the grades ahead of mine.

My parents encouraged my achievements at school just as they equally encouraged my brothers' and sisters' successes, whether they were in sports or music or anything else in which one of us excelled. Today when I win a case (or even a race) I look forward to calling home and receiving the same encouragement and support.

During the years I was growing up, I often spent weeks with my maternal grandparents on their small farm. They were kind, hard-working people. Now when I look out at our strawberry fields, I often remember waking up early on June mornings and seeing them already at work in their strawberry patch.

When I was 10, my parents bought a livestock feed business in addition to the farm. My father, who at 18 had started as a farm hand with no money, greatly valued his independence, and the new business helped insure that. Although I now work at a salaried job, I share my father's feeling. I like being a manager in the legal services office partially because I want to have as much control as possible over my work and working environment.

I never met a lawyer until I was an adult, but arguments over politics were a way of life in my family, and I soon joined them. If anything foreshadowed my eventual career as a lawyer during those years, it was the books and the arguments.

And if those were any forecast of a legal career, another influence was at work which helped determine the path my legal career would take. My parents believed in giving time for causes that were important to them. Dad spent countless hours working on the reorganization and consolidation of the country school districts. I learned early that one was expected to spend time on what he or she believed in. And while my parents and my three living grandparents loved me and influenced me, I was also deeply influenced by my father's father who had died 20 years before I was born. He was a state organizer for the National Farmers Union during its early years in Nebraska. Throughout the years that my father was growing up, until his death when my father was 13, my grandfather continued as an organizer in three or four midwestern states. Hanging on my wall at home is a photograph of a handbill from one of his speeches in 1915 or 1916. The handbill proclaims that it is the purpose of the National Farmers Union to work for "equal justice to all communities and equity for all classes and occupations." I grew up hearing stories of his commitment to the cooperative movement and to justice.

During high school, I watched and admired the activities of the civil rights movement from a great distance. When I heard a local priest describe the march to Selma, I knew I wanted to be like those who were in the ranks of that movement.

By the time I finished high school, I was anxious to leave home. My teenage years had been no more nor less eventful than those of anyone else, but I wanted new friends, new teachers, and new things to read. In 1966, despite my parents' reluctance that I go so far from home, I started college at Michigan State University. I chose that school because Michigan State did extensive recruiting of National Merit Scholars, and also because my uncle was a professor of agricultural economics there.

As a member of the Honors College, I was in advanced classes and small seminars from my first semester. In fact, I found exactly what I had been seeking—teachers who could stimulate my intellectual growth and friends who were also genuinely interested in learning.

I soon discovered, however, that while Michigan State was in fact providing me the sort of education I wanted, the politics of a university sometimes run counter to good education. The most stimulating of my teachers during that first year was fired despite the fact that he was perhaps the best teacher in the department and editor of the only literary journal on campus. I joined the demonstrators then, and later, after the firings of other inspiring but non-conformist faculty.

Of much more consequence than firings on a college campus was the intensification of the Vietnam War. My brother was in Vietnam, and I began college with, at best, confused feelings and thoughts about the war. Freed from the pro-war sentiment of a small town, I began to question, and to read. By the end of my first year, I had joined the anti-war movement and I remained active in it for several years.

The women's movement was in its infancy on campus. Men held most of the student government positions, headed up the regular student activities, as well as the anti-war movement, and led the demonstrations. But again I began to listen, think, and learn, and by the end of my college career I identified myself as a feminist. Although I was only occasionally active in women's groups, the tremendous support of women for their sisters that grew up during that movement was very important to me.

In January 1968, halfway through college, I met Jim Hunsley, a graduate student in biochemistry. He was the iconoclastic son of an Illinois coal mining family, who had put himself through college and was now studying on an assistantship in his department. Within a few weeks we were spending most of our free time together. I was first attracted to him by the variety and depth of his interests. He had been intensely interested in music in college and introduced me to classical and twentieth century music. He was a terrific cook as well, and food was an interest we shared. We also found that we shared some long-term goals: Although we both expected to have professional careers, we explored the idea of combining those careers in some way with our mutual interest in farming. Jim was looking for an independent, career-oriented woman with whom to share his life. I was not looking for a serious relationship then, but within a short time, I realized that having found Jim, I had no intention of separating from him when we finished school. The decision to make a commitment to him was perhaps the easiest of my life. In December 1968, when I was 19, we were married in the Lansing City Hall in the presence of two witnesses. We followed the ceremony with a meal at a Chinese restaurant and settled into a tiny apartment to finish our last year at Michigan State.

I graduated nine months later with honors in political science. Throughout college I had studied the history and economics of third world countries. By the time I graduated, I had developed a strong interest in Chinese studies. Jim finished his Ph.D. a few months later, and we moved to Cambridge, Massachusetts. Jim had a postdoctoral fellowship there in the Biological Laboratories at Harvard. I was hoping for admission to the Chinese studies program there. By then I was 21, and the idea of law school had not yet crossed my mind.

Once at Harvard, I took a job in the Widener Library, having worked throughout college as an assistant in the Labor and Industrial Relations Library at Michigan State. I was deeply disappointed a few weeks later when I learned I was rejected from the Chinese studies program, at least partially because I had become interested in Chinese studies so late in my college career that I had no language training. I began taking a night course in Chinese with the idea of applying for graduate school again the following year.

At the same time, however, I was beginning to have doubts. I had seen enough of academics through Jim's work to know the difficulties of finding employment after graduate school. I also was not at all sure that I was interested in teaching or, although I liked historical research, in spending my professional life writing papers. I walked past the Harvard Law School on my way to work every morning, and I began to meet law students in the library. I was more awed by the law school than I was by the rest of Harvard University, but as I met students there, I began to realize that they seemed neither brighter nor more articulate than I. It is hard to remember now whether it was Jim or I who first thought that I should try law school. I hedged my bets, applied to both law school and graduate school, and took the LSAT exams at the last possible moment.

By the time I began to receive acceptances from law schools, I was convinced that law would be more to my liking than academics. It seemed to me that a law degree would be much more useful than a Ph.D. if one wanted to participate actively in the struggles against sexism, racism, and poverty.

Although by then I was sure about law school, I was less sure about Harvard. Its law school had a reputation that would terrify anyone, especially someone still somewhat lacking in confidence.

And my first contact with the law school after I was accepted was less than encouraging. Jim's salary was small, and my own earnings and savings were not adequate for law school expenses; the financial aid office announced that I was ineligible for a scholarship. They counted Jim's income as mine—but not his debts to pay off educational loans. I was furious. Other than the fact that it seemed irrational, it appeared to me that more women than men would get caught in this bind. I objected and was met with the most indifferent of responses. I could come to Harvard without financial aid or I could go somewhere else. I was practical enough to choose Harvard but I hardly felt welcome as I began.

But then, as throughout law school, I received support from those around me. A friend of mine from college, a woman in her forties with an established career, called and offered to help. She said she would like to send me a check every month while I was in law school to help with my living expenses. The money was not a loan. She told me that she was giving me the money because she was convinced I would use my law degree to the benefit of those most desperately in need of legal help. I was surprised, pleased, and very grateful. For not only did the money help me get through law school but the confidence others had in me fueled my own.

And certainly I needed all the moral support I could get during that first year. I had the not uncommon experience of being terrified. Twelve percent of my class were women—distinctly a minority and a novelty. Tension ran high for all students, male and female, throughout the year because huge law school classes meant that any one student was seldom called upon, so no one became comfortable speaking in class. I think women participated less than men in the classroom discussions that first year, and it certainly seemed that people were unusually attentive when a woman was called on. Could it really be that I was called on only a half-dozen times that entire first year and that, despite the rarity of that occurrence, I always hated going to some courses? Did I really wake up sick in the morning dreading class? At that time, a student's entire grades for the year were based on the exams at the end of the year. When I finally had my grades, and realized I had done well enough, I breathed a sigh of relief and realized that—whatever happened in my final two years of law school—I could never care so much about school again.

As I struggled through that first year, my career goals did not become much more focused. But I had found other people whose intentions were similar to mine, and I heard about the growing legal aid movement in the United States. I also heard, however, that one could accomplish little at legal aid offices.

At the beginning of my second year, I applied to be a member of the Harvard Legal Aid Bureau, the school's student-run, volunteer legal services office which was founded in 1912. To be eligible, one had to make a two-year commitment to be on the staff 20 hours a week. That year, as most years, there were more applicants than openings, and I was chosen by lottery. I also signed up for a clinical course so that I would have supervision and training while I began working in student legal services. Again, there were more applicants than openings, but a few additional openings were created under intense pressure by the students. I found myself beginning to practice law.

The Legal Aid Bureau involved that year approximately 60 second- and third-year students. Much of the supervision was provided by the third-year students. Except for those in the clinical course, the members of the bureau relied on occasional help from an attorney with the Legal Aid Society in Boston. We had two tiny interview rooms, and a variety of old typewriters which we used to produce our own pleadings and briefs. We had no copying machines and no secretaries. We did have Elizabeth Allebach, the administrative director who held (and still holds) the bureau together. But despite the cramped quarters and the less than adequate supervision provided, the bureau rapidly became the most important part of law school to me. During those two years, two teaching fellows, John Bowman and Valerie Vanaman, both former legal aid attorneys, did what they could to help us practice high quality law under extremely trying circumstances.

And almost from the day I walked in the door, I knew that I had found my career. The work was challenging, complex, and exciting. The victories came often enough to compensate for the losses. Our clients desperately needed help and, with the guidance of our teaching fellows, we began to realize that we could in fact provide it. I began to make weekly bus trips to Dorchester (Mass.) to interview clients at the offices of a tenants' association. I appeared in the new Boston Housing Court, and was soon involved in a lawsuit regarding conditions at a Dorchester apartment house. While I became familiar with federal housing legislation, other friends at the bureau began making their way through the maze of welfare laws and regulations. Even in those beginning days, I knew that there was nothing simple about legal aid work.

I also learned then how important the administration of a legal assistance program is to the quality of the services provided. At the end of my second year, I was elected president of the Legal Aid Bureau and, with the other members of the student board of directors, tried to obtain more support from the law school, especially better supervision by practicing attorneys. Our efforts were partially successful although lack of support continued to be an issue at the bureau for several years.

By the middle of my third year, my attention was, like most other law students, focused on obtaining a job. For me that meant obtaining a legal services position in an office where I would be able to do high quality and meaningful work for my clients. Fortunately, I had guidance as to what that office should be like. The teaching fellows at the bureau helped me compose a list of things to look for when I visited offices—including years of experience and type of work of the attorneys in the office, caseload control, the amount of specialization, and even the existence of dictaphones and decent typewriters. The location of the office was perhaps the least important factor to me. I had already decided that I would prefer to move back to the Midwest, both because my family was there and because I believed there were more areas in the Midwest where the legal services offices were relatively new and many important issues had not been litigated. Jim was looking at the same time for an academic position. The scarcity of those jobs meant that we would probably move wherever he received a good offer, so long as I could find what I was looking for in the same area.

After Jim received an offer from St. Louis University School of Medicine, I went job hunting in St. Louis and East St. Louis. The East St. Louis Office of Land of Lincoln Legal Assistance seemed right for me. There were two attorneys, George Parker and John O'Brien, with good legal services experience; the other criteria on my list were also met. I also interviewed at law firms and government agencies in St. Louis. Those interviews were helpful to me in confirming what I already believed—that the legal services job was the one I really wanted.

When I accepted the position in East St. Louis, I had already been told of the extreme poverty as well as the "white flight" from the city over the previous two decades. While the office served the entire county, a majority of our clients did come from East St. Louis itself. And while I had become familiar with urban poverty during my two years at the legal aid bureau, I still knew that work in a city as economically depressed as East St. Louis would be extremely difficult.

East St. Louis, a city of slightly over 50,000 people, has changed in the last 20 years from an ethnically diverse population to one that is over 90 percent black. During that time, the industries and companies that were the life blood of the city left one by one. As a result, even by 1974 when I started, East St. Louis was a city where official unemployment statistics had absolutely no meaning. Many residents had been looking for work so long that they had given up. Over 60 percent of the population existed on government assistance. The town had a long-time reputation for corruption in politics, and when the white politicians fled, along with the rest of the white population in the sixties, they left behind a city drained of most of its resources. It was, and is, a city where the most frequent optimistic comment is that "things can get no worse." In 1974, it was a city where a new legal services lawyer had to wonder whether it was possible to make the slightest bit of difference.

Initially my job was to become familiar with the community and its institutions and to begin serving the many individual clients who came to our doors. I began working in consumer law while also taking on some public housing cases. Since one of my requirements for an office was that I be allowed to concentrate my practice in a few areas of law, the arrangement was exactly what I wanted.

The obstacles I faced were not solely those of a young legal services lawyer beginning practice in an extraordinarily depressed community. I found that I was one of only two or three women practicing law in the entire county. There were not (and still are not) any women judges. There were no women in private practice. The one other female attorney in our office left shortly after I came. The only other active woman practitioner was in criminal law. There was no doubt that when I walked into the courtroom, I walked into a man's world. And worse than the courtroom were the judge's chambers—the "back room." The combination of being a woman from the legal aid office and from an out-of-state law school, was almost an insurmountable obstacle to joining in small talk. And I knew, of course, that joining in was important. In the midst of such conversation, cases are discussed, settlements are reached, and judges begin to form their opinions about cases. I compensated in the only way I knew how, by writing better briefs, by preparing more for my cases, by thinking more about my negotiations. All that did give me enough advantage to make me feel I was serving my clients well. But I still knew the casual conversations were important, and, over the years, I and some other members of our office have gradually built up relationships with judges and other attorneys so that we, too, can sometimes use the judges' chambers to our advantage.

The "back room," of course, did not just include the conference rooms and judge's chambers at court. It also included other places where lawyers congregate, such as bar association meetings. When I began practicing in East St. Louis, the bar association had the reputation of being a men's club. If one were male, and liked to drink, the meetings were a good place for entertainment. But even the male members of our office felt distinctly unwelcome and didn't attend. I never even considered making an appearance. That too has changed.

About two years ago, women began attending the meetings regularly. I remember during the first six or seven I attended, the speaker or the president or another member would always make some remark about the fact that there were women present. But in the last year, those remarks have become less and less frequent. When I was elected this spring to the board of directors of the Bar Association as its first woman member, I was personally glad because it gave me the opportunity to discuss regularly legal aid and *pro bono* issues with the other officers of the bar. But it was also a milestone for women in the county whose presence here has finally been acknowledged.

Because there were no role models in St. Clair County when I moved there, it was hard to even know what to wear. In court, I dressed mostly in conservative pant suits, and no one ever commented. Once I argued before the appellate court dressed in a three piece wool pant suit. Only years later did I learn from a former clerk of one of the judges that another judge on the panel, seeing that I was dressed in pants rather than a skirt, had insisted that I not be allowed to argue. He was finally dissuaded by the other members of the panel. I hope my attire did not influence the outcome of that case, but I have sometimes wondered. It is hard to practice when men set the protocol, and even more so, when women have no way of knowing what it is.

During that early time, I relied on support from two of the male attorneys in the office, as well as on the very strong support and encouragement I received from Jim. For a brief period, another woman worked in the office, but she found herself unable to cope with the tensions of practice and left. We advertised for a new attorney. I still remember the distress I felt on the day that the directing attorney told me he had narrowed down the choice to two candidates, and that he had decided the man was the better candidate. My distress was not at his decision. I had also interviewed both candidates and believed he was right. Rather, I just became overwhelmingly aware of how much I would prefer to have another woman attorney practicing in the office. I persuaded the director to hold off on a hiring decision for a few more days. During that time a well-qualified, female, former legal services attorney applied and was hired. My sense of relief was intense.

Now, of the seven staff attorneys who work in this office, five are women. In St. Clair County, there are at least 20 women practicing, including a number in private firms. While it is true that we are still a relative rarity, gradually the novelty wears off, and practicing law becomes easier.

During those first few years, I continued to serve large numbers of clients. As I did so, I also began to meet leaders of poor people's groups in the community. Those contacts became increasingly useful as the leaders came to know that when an issue seriously affected a number of their members, they could call on me for assistance. I also began to recognize those issues which were of most importance to the client community in East St. Louis. For example, I represented a number of poor people in a series of utility rate increase cases. Although to some extent poor people share the common residential concern of holding prices down, they are most affected by issues such as minimum charges. One cannot simply argue poverty when representing clients in a rate proceeding; it is necessary to understand economics and to produce expert witnesses who can justify rate structures most favorable to low-income people. Gradually I acquired that knowledge and contacts with experts that allowed my office to have some success in the rate increase cases.

Having seen dozens of individual clients with complaints about admissions to the local housing authority, I filed a class action on their behalf alleging that admissions were being made in an arbitrary and capricious manner. Proving the case required again the use of expert witnesses and a computer analysis of the admissions made as compared to those which would have been made if the written policies had been followed. At the successful conclusion of that case, I realized my skills as a litigator had continued to improve. I felt more and more confident of my ability to handle major lawsuits.

But the major legal challenge of my legal services career came upon me suddenly. A newspaper article announced one of the two hospitals in town would be closed by its white owners, who had recently finished building a new hospital in the white suburbs. Not only was the hospital needed in our community; 400 jobs would be lost if the hospital closed.

A number of poor people asked me to represent them in their efforts to keep the hospital open. The case required a combined strategy with black doctors, community leaders, politicians, and the hospital service employees' union. The strategy we jointly developed was to file a civil rights complaint with the Office of Civil Rights of the U.S. Department of Health and Human Services in which we argued that the owners were discriminating against blacks by depriving them of access to health care. At the same time we opposed the closing of the hospital in hearings before the local Health Systems Agency.

Dan Mulvaney, an attorney from our Alton office, and I took responsibility for finding experts and presenting data at the Health Systems Agency while community people and union members organized testimony for public hearings. Dan, Sandy Newman of the Center for Law and Social Policy in Washington, D. C., and I initiated and continued contacts with the Office of Civil Rights investigators, introducing them to possible witnesses, analyzing their data and pointing out what additional information they needed.

The activity was varied and intense. After the Office of Civil Rights made a preliminary determination that there had been a civil rights violation, the board of the Health Systems Agency voted against allowing the hospital to close. The white owners of the hospital agreed to deed the hospital to a new corporation made up of black doctors and community leaders, and to give that group $300,000 to help meet the hospital's immediate needs.

The fight consumed six months, but the hospital remains open today. It is still struggling, as are most hospitals located in low-income communities, but it has recently rehabilitated one wing and received a grant to update its ambulatory care facilities. I remember clearly the enormous rapport I felt with members of the community as I addressed the public hearing on the proposed closing, and I remember with warmth the ceremony at the Baptist church honoring those of us who had participated in the struggle. If ever I need to remind myself of why it is worthwhile to continue working in legal services, I need only drive past the open doors of Community Hospital.

While my first few years of lawyering were focused entirely on improving my own skills and the quality of my work, I later began to work on legal services issues on the national level. In 1977, I was elected to the National Steering Committee of the Project Advisory

Group (PAG), an organization of legal services directors, staff, and clients.

I worked on the PAG national committee for only one year. While it was stimulating and satisfying to meet legal services people from throughout the country and share information and ideas, I found it very difficult at the same time to be a full-time legal services lawyer with many clients, to manage the office, and to spend enough time at home with my husband.

When I became directing attorney of our office in 1978, administrative work began to take more of my time. Within our office I was expected to supervise, evaluate, and be responsible for the quality of the legal work. In addition, I was responsible for recommendations on hiring and, if necessary, firing of employees, although final decisions were made by our executive director.

And of course there are dozens of smaller administrative duties—ranging from meetings with the advisory council to distribution of secretarial work. Some duties can be delegated, but all can rebound if there is a snafu.

My feelings about administrative work have varied over the years, but now they are favorable. I've learned that it can be very enjoyable to hire and train a promising new attorney. It is also satisfying to review the past year, knowing that we have organized the office to make good use of very scarce resources and have accomplished much of what we planned.

At other times, administrative work has seemed burdensome and draining. That is particularly the case when I have had to work with, evaluate, and eventually fire an unsatisfactory employee. While it may be necessary, it can also be extremely unpleasant—especially if one must testify at hearings concerning the firing. But I don't believe it was any harder (or easier) to perform this role because I am a woman.

I have little to say about my supervision of male attorneys—and perhaps that says less about me than about the men in legal services. Problems that have arisen don't seem to be sex-role problems, and I have enjoyed working with male attorneys in the office as much as with female ones.

My supervisor, since I became a directing attorney, is Joseph Bartylak, the director of the program. He has intervened in our particular office only when asked, and when I have had problems, he has been a source of tremendous assistance. The autonomy allowed me has made it easier to develop as a manager and as a lawyer.

As Land of Lincoln expanded to serve 65 counties in central and southern Illinois, I gradually became more involved in program-wide coordination and administration. I became chairperson of the housing committee of the program, an informal group of attorneys who met to exchange ideas, report on current cases, provide training to newer lawyers and to co-counsel difficult cases. My interest in the training of new lawyers also led me to become the coordinator for new lawyers' training for our program for two years.

When a staff committee was formed to advise the program director and board on a variety of issues (recruitment, benefits, evaluations, etc.), I became the directing attorney representative and then the chairperson. In 1981 and 1983, staff and client committees were formed to plan Land of Lincoln's response to national funding reductions. I chaired both the 1981 and the 1983 cutback committees. It cannot be said to be satisfying to write reports recommending closings of offices and terminations of staff. But it was satisfying as chairperson, to see some consensus emerging and to see the program react to the funding crisis in a way which will allow us to keep our basic structure intact as we wait for better times. No matter how unpleasant a decision will be, I prefer, if it will affect the delivery of legal services to clients in our area, that I be involved in the decision-making. And in legal services, it is possible to be involved if one is willing to spend the time and the emotional energy confronting the issues.

Despite tensions created by being both a lawyer and a manager, I have found it possible to combine office and program-wide administration with litigation and with service to community groups. And during the last several years I have found it possible to spend more time on other interests.

By 1979, Jim had become increasingly dissatisfied with academics. We had been living in a small town, spending time rehabilitating an old house and filling our acre lot with gardens and more trees. As our interest in horticulture increased, our earlier plans to move some day to a farm began to seem more realistic. In 1979 we decided that the time had come, if ever, for Jim to make a career change. He resigned as a faculty member, and we purchased a small farm with an even older house. The house had not been lived in for several years and the yard and fields were overgrown with weeds and brush. Gradually, we have begun to transform it into our pick-your-own berry and vegetable farm. While my input has been somewhat minimal compared to Jim's, I have put in gardens and trees, cleared fences, done the accounting, and helped with berry sales during my vacations from work.

In some ways, although the business has resulted in more work and fatigue, it has also been helpful in permitting me to remain in legal services. "Burnout" is the term usually used to describe the condition reached by legal services and other social services workers if the rewards are too few, the work too hard, the clients too demanding, and the support so little that one can no longer go on working. I suspect there are few of us who haven't at least had occasional moments of burnout, but for me they have been momentary in part because I find that my farm work provides a refreshing balance.

I have always had other interests as well: reading (especially fiction by women authors ranging from Doris Lessing to Ursula LeGuin), cooking, listening to fiddle music, practicing Yoga, and running. Those activities have helped me live with the stress which is part of my life as an attorney.

As I end my ninth year of legal services work in East St. Louis, I have no regrets about my decision to come here, nor do I have any desire to leave. To me, the work I do for clients is still extremely interesting and the successes, whether on behalf of one client or hundreds, are frequent enough to make me feel that I am accomplishing something.

There are a number of things that have allowed me to remain a career legal services attorney. Perhaps the most important factor was my early decision to only work at a legal aid office at which I would have enough support, and enough autonomy, to develop professionally as an attorney and to be able to provide high quality legal services to my clients.

It has also been helpful to me that legal services work is so varied. When one becomes tired of the details of a complex case that has been going on for years, it is good to be able to turn to the defense of a relatively simple mortgage foreclosure action and see immediate results. When litigation appears non-productive, it is satisfying to be able to represent low-income community groups in non-litigation activities which sometimes bring more results. And when my own cases seem frustrating, I can turn to the problems of our office and try to develop ways to provide as much service as possible without making heavier demands on staff.

We have now developed an office of seven attorneys which I would be willing to match in legal skills and dedication against any law firm of comparable size in the country. Three of us have been in legal services for nine years or more, and the rest from one to five years. Though friendships become strained, and tensions emerge even in a close and supportive office, I think we have all assisted each other in staying on in legal services work.

In sum, legal services has meant for me the opportunity to do complex legal work on behalf of people who desperately need it. I believe that I have assisted my clients in obtaining access to justice, and as a result of that access, they have had—at least on some occasions—more say in their communities and more influence over the institutions that affect them. Legal services to the poor is under attack nationally, but as long as Congress, the legal profession, and the American people continue to remain committed to the ideal of equal access to justice, I expect to remain a legal services attorney.

CHAPTER 6

AS PUBLIC INTEREST LAWYER:
A Sense of Purpose

BY MARCIA D. GREENBERGER

Julie Wiatt

MARCIA D. GREENBERGER

MARCIA D. GREENBERGER

National Women's Law Center
Washington, D.C.

Education

J.D., University of Pennsylvania Law School, 1970, cum laude

A.B., University of Pennsylvania, 1967, Phi Gamma Mu National Honor Society (history)

Experience

Managing Attorney, National Women's Law Center, 1981-present

Founder, Women's Rights Project, Center for Law and Social Policy, Washington, D.C., 1972-1981

Political Director, New England Region McGovern for President Campaign, August 1972-November 1972

Associate, Caplin and Drysdale, Washington, D.C., 1970-1972

Part-time Law Clerk, Ballard, Spahr, Andrews and Ingersoll, Philadelphia, 1969-1970

Summer Law Clerk, Regional Counsel, Internal Revenue Service, Philadelphia, summer 1969

Professional Activities

Admitted to practice in Washington, D.C., 1970

Member, Board of Directors, National Health Law Program, Inc., 1982-present

Member, Board of Directors, Federation of Organizations for Professional Women, 1982-present

Member, Advisory Committee, Disability Rights Education and Defense Fund, 1981-present

Member, Board of Directors, Black Student Fund, 1980-present

Member, Hearing Committee, Board of Professional Responsibility of the District of Columbia Bar, 1979-present

Member, District of Columbia Bar Committee on Public Service Activities, 1979-present

Member, Federation of Women Lawyers Judicial Screening Project, 1977-present

Member, District of Columbia Bar Ethics Committee, 1980-1983

Member, Board of Governors, Health Law Forum, American Bar Association, 1979-1982

Chairperson, Consumer Protection Committee of the Administrative Law Section, American Bar Association, 1980; Vice-Chair, 1981

Member, Advisory Working Group, Office of Technological Assessment, United States Congress on Study of Extension of Patent Term and the Pharmaceutical Industry, 1981

Member, Joint Commission on Prescription Drug Use, 1976-1980

Member, Advisory Panel to General Accounting Office review of FDA Drug Regulation Process, 1980

Member, Advisory Panel to American College of Obstetrics and Gynecology on Development of Guidelines for Physicians on Pregnancy and Work, 1976

Publications

Sex Discrimination in Education: Legal Rights and Remedies, 1983 (co-authored with Campbell, Kohn and Wilcher)

"The Effectiveness of Federal Laws Prohibiting Sex Discrimination in Employment in the United States," in Ratner, ed., *Equal Employment Policy for Women,* 1979

"Legal Remedies Beyond Title VII to Combat Sex Discrimination in Employment," in Kahn, ed., *Women in the U.S. Labor Force,* 1979 (co-authored with Gutmann)

"A Consumer Advocate's View of the FDA's Procedures and Practices," 32 *Food, Drug Cosmetic Law Journal* 293, 1977

"The Progeny of *Gelduldig v. Aiello:* Can Employers Really Assume Pregnancy is Unrelated to Sex?" 1 *Employee Relations Law Journal* 41, 1975 (co-authored with Schiffer)

Personal

Born: April 24, 1946, Philadelphia, Pa.

Married: 1969

Children: Two, born in 1974 and 1978

Chapter 6

AS PUBLIC INTEREST LAWYER: A SENSE OF PURPOSE

BY MARCIA D. GREENBERGER

I have been a lawyer for 13 years. Eleven of those years have been spent working on women's rights. In looking back, and thinking about how I chose my work, I realize that in many ways, my career has been a product of changing times for and expectations about women.

I graduated from high school in 1963, with most of my female peers assuming that their adult responsibilities would center around marriage and children. Young women were urged to view a career as important only in a limited way—to rely upon until their husbands established a career, and to fall back on in the event that crisis struck and they had to support themselves and their children. Not much thought was given to possible jobs beyond those traditionally held by women.

Yet, at the same time, the Kennedy years, which overlapped with much of the time I was in high school, had an enormous impact on us as well. Washington, D.C. in general, and government jobs in particular, seemed exciting and glamorous. Although I did not see women holding those jobs, I remember unfocused but fervent discussions about how wonderful it would be to become a part of that world.

The aura of glamour diminished, but social activism of the middle and late sixties—when I was in college and law school—intensified my belief that government could make an enormous difference in people's lives. My generation of students thought that they personally had a role in changing things—not only was business-as-usual subject to examination, but change was warranted. And producing that change was up to us.

I loved college. I loved the courses and the challenge, but I also loved the dynamism on campus during those years. We had a sense of real power, marching and sitting in college buildings, expressing our views on issues ranging from saving trees to the Vietnam War. The women students were definitely a part of the action, if not quite as free to participate as the men. The women had a chance to shine in classes as well—but again, not quite to the same degree as the men. I remember taking a course in economics, and being one of very few women in the class. We felt somewhat conspicuous, and tended to be more careful before participating in class discussions. But we had a sense of achievement when we did well, and we learned that we could succeed in a male setting.

I was a history major in college. By the time I was a senior, I had focused more clearly on my career plans. To me, the perfect job would have been as a college professor. News had not yet hit about a contracting job market in higher education, and the best and brightest seemed headed toward Ph.D.s, teaching, and research careers.

However, one of the most prestigious professors in the history department, who was also my advisor, told me it was a mistake for a woman to go to graduate school in history. He warned me that chances were I would get married before I ever got my Ph.D., and then I would drop out. My job prospects would be no better than had I not gone to graduate school at all. I valued his advice, even though I wished he were more encouraging about employment possibilities for women in higher education. Yet the history department had just hired a young woman as an assistant professor, so I had tangible proof it could be done. I applied to graduate school in history despite my advisor's warnings.

At the same time, two of my female friends were thinking about law school, and I went with them to take the law school aptitude tests. Several men came up to the three of us before the test started and asked how we could take the test and compete with men who "really needed" to get into law school. Not only was it assumed that men needed a law career more than women, but at that time law school attendance was still grounds for a military deferment. I was taken aback at the blatant hostility, and wondered about what kind of reception I would receive if I did go to law school.

Nonetheless, law school made a lot of sense to me. It was good training for a public policy job, and with a law degree teaching was still a possibility. My friends and I encouraged each other, and we all decided to give it a try. Two of us started at the University of Pennsylvania Law School together. Having a ready friend and ally made my adjustment there incalculably easier.

Only 12 women ultimately graduated in my law school class. We were totally conspicuous. The fact of being different and having to explain and justify to my classmates why I was in law school, especially in the first year, was something I accepted, although never appreciated.

Some professors never called on us. Others took a different tack. My criminal law professor, for example, saved all the rape cases for the women—it was a great source of amusement in class to require the women to review the details of the rape and the defenses raised.

But the treatment of women in law school was not an issue that many discussed or viewed as a problem. Rather, we were preoccupied by two other major issues of the time—enormous student unrest and demonstrations over the Vietnam War, and student idealism about law careers devoted to public service. Much has been written about student activism of the sixties and early seventies. Suffice it to say that this activism permeated the law school, and provided an atmosphere congenial to and supportive of my aspirations for public service.

Law firms recognized the interests of many of the law students. They recruited members of our class by offering substantial opportunities for *pro bono* work in combination with the private firms' traditional practice. A number of law students shunned private practice altogether as dull, unchallenging, and socially unproductive work, although many of them are in firms now. In our class there was relatively little concern about finding a job—the real question for many was finding the right job.

I tended to share the views of those students who were looking for work directly connected with social reform. I doubted that commercial private practice was suited to my interests. Therefore, I was surprised to find that one of the courses I enjoyed the most was on taxation. The issues were intellectually challenging and the policy judgments reflected in the federal tax laws were fascinating to me.

The summer after my second year in law school I worked in the regional counsel's office of the Internal Revenue Service. During my third year, I decided to try private practice, and worked as a part-time law clerk for a large, private firm. I was expected to rotate through all of the departments in the firm, but started with the tax department and enjoyed the work so much that it was agreed I would stay there throughout the year.

I got married while in law school—to another law student—and my husband and I decided to move to Washington, D.C. after graduation. I had not given up my idea of a public policy job, but had difficulty finding one. The Nixon Administration had just begun, and many of the government agencies I was most interested in were in a state of flux. Not knowing of many alternatives, I interviewed for jobs with several law firms. In a number of cases, the firms had never hired women lawyers. One senior partner told me that partners in his firm hesitated to hire a woman lawyer because they expected their lawyers to work late. The firm did not believe that a woman should stay late at night given the purported dangers of crime in Washington. No explanation was offered as to why it was acceptable for female secretaries to work late.

I did join a relatively small firm specializing in tax law—Caplin and Drysdale—and stayed for two years. I was the first woman lawyer the firm had hired; they hired a second woman the next year. I enjoyed the firm, and learned an enormous amount during the time I was there. I liked the challenge of working through the issues, and the people in the firm itself. But I still wanted a chance to work on public policy issues. Although the firm supported *pro bono* activities in which I participated, the time available was, of course, limited.

After I had been at Caplin and Drysdale for two years, I learned of job openings at the Center for Law and Social Policy—one of the first "public interest" law firms, started in 1969. The Center's purpose was to provide legal counsel to previously underrepresented groups, as well as to engage in public policy analysis. Because of its Washington location, its primary emphasis was on federal government policies and practices affecting the groups the Center represented.

The Center worked in a number of areas, ranging from environmental issues to consumer protection to mental health. At the urging of the secretaries at the Center, it was then considering taking on women's rights issues. The prospect of working on women's rights was particularly appealing to me.

The 1972 presidential election was also heating up at the time. The chance to be a part of a presidential campaign seemed like the fulfillment of my high school aspirations. I left Caplin and Drysdale to work in the McGovern campaign, and eventually was in charge of coordinating efforts in the northeastern states. At the same time, I also accepted a job at the Center to work on women's rights, and arranged to begin after the campaign was over.

By this point in 1972, expectations for women had changed dramatically from those which prevailed when I began college. As was true for growing numbers of women, work was an integral part of my life. My job was not a temporary phenomenon to be dropped to accommodate family needs. Fortunately, my husband always valued my career, and understood its demands. I never felt that I had to choose between a career and my personal life.

I began my job at the Center, excited not only at the prospect of going back to practicing law after several months of working in a political campaign, but also at the chance to work full-time on issues of great importance to me. My experiences in a political campaign demonstrated to me, in fact, that I enjoyed the practice of law and that combining law practice with work on social reform was ideal.

From the start, I loved my job at the Center. It was, and still is, a unique and terrific place. It has provided unparalleled flexibility, not only to select specific issues for attention, but also to combine litigation, federal agency advocacy, writing, and work on Capitol Hill. The autonomy, combined with the chance to handle important issues, was difficult for a young lawyer like myself to duplicate elsewhere.

There was an aspect of teaching involved in the job as well, which I also valued. The Center had a law student intern program. Students from Yale, University of Pennsylvania, University of Michigan,

Stanford and U.C.L.A. came to the Center for a semester. All of the lawyers supervised the students' work, and gave seminars.

The Center's atmosphere also suited me. It was informal, but there was no laxness in connection with our work. The lawyers truly enjoyed working with each other, and although I was only one of two women lawyers at the Center when I began, I was used to being in the minority.

My first Center assignment reflects the lack of understanding of women's issues that even the public interest bar had at the time. Although I was the first full-time, paid, public interest lawyer in Washington to work on women's rights, I was asked to write a paper assessing whether there was enough work to keep me busy full time, and outlining projects I might undertake. To the Center's credit, once I began to discuss issues which needed to be addressed, everyone agreed it would be far more productive to begin work immediately and dispense with writing a paper justifying my working full-time on women's rights.

So I began. From the first, the range of issues was enormous, and it became clear that one lawyer could not even scratch the surface. I worked on an employment discrimination case, then pending in district court, in which union lawyers challenged an employer's then common practice of excluding pregnancy-related disabilities from its employee disability plan. The case, *General Electric v. Gilbert,*, ultimately reached the Supreme Court, and the exclusion was declared to be legal. Congress then amended the law prohibiting sex discrimination in employment, Title VII of the Civil Rights Act of 1964, to outlaw discrimination on the basis of pregnancy—thereby requiring employers to treat pregnancy like any other physical condition. We were active in the legislative effort to amend Title VII to provide this protection.

With a physician from Yale University Medical School, I interviewed women in rural Tennessee who unknowingly had been given an experimental birth control drug. I then testified in highly publicized Senate hearings regarding the abuses involved in the use of the drug and suggested protections needed to avoid a recurrence. I also began work with several women's groups preparing a lawsuit against the federal government for failure to enforce sex discrimination laws in schools.

The work was exciting and rewarding. The women involved in women's rights issues, although few in number, were bright and dedicated. The major problem was the limitation on the amount of work that could be done with only one Center lawyer assigned to women's rights. The answer seemed simple in the expansive days of the early seventies: We would create a Women's Rights Project and raise funds from foundations to hire a second, and hopefully, eventually a third lawyer. I went off to New York with the director of the Center, with no idea then of how often I would repeat New York fundraising trips in the future.

In 1973, we did in fact create the Women's Rights Project of the Center with its own advisory board, received specific funding for the Project, and hired a second lawyer. What a difference it made having someone to work with on a full-time basis. The issues we addressed continued to expand, from breast cancer experiments to treatment of women in the military to discrimination in insurance.

My job was all I could hope for. It was varied in the types of work we did, the people with whom we worked, and the issues we addressed. The Center was supportive of our work, providing wide latitude to take on the projects we selected. Our advisory board was comprised of individuals committed to women's rights and extremely knowledgeable in a number of fields. They were a wonderful resource to draw upon, and continued to be a mainstay to the organization.

I did not expect the Center to offer lifetime employment in the way that a private firm might, but I was happy to exchange security for the advantages the Center did offer. In 1974, after I had been at the Center for a year and a half, and had seen the Women's Rights Project established, my first child was born. I was comfortable at the Center, and was confident that it would provide me flexibility to handle my new child care responsibilities. But before my daughter was born, I didn't have a clue as to how it would all actually work out.

In fact, circumstances worked in our favor far more than is true for many working couples. We were able to secure excellent child care, and the Center was willing to adjust to my need for a flexible schedule to accommodate my new demands. I had my second child in 1978, and continued following the same routine.

That is not to say that combining children and a career is easy, even under what I consider to be close to ideal circumstances. The balance is always tenuous at best. There is simply not enough time to take on all of the women's rights issues that need attention, or enough time to be with my daughters as much as I would like. However, I am not sure that either my work or my daughters have suffered as much as I from the feeling of being torn between the two.

In fact, the Women's Rights Project continued to grow despite a general contraction of public interest activities in the 1970's. In 1975, we were able to secure enough additional funds to add a third lawyer, and a fourth in 1979.

By 1981, the Project had expanded and matured to the point where it could better function as an independent organization—and it became the National Women's Law Center. NWLC continues a close relationship with the Center for Law and Social Policy—we have joint responsibility for our ongoing student program and share several employees. NWLC now has a staff of 14, including six lawyers, and generally trains about nine law students a year. In fact, NWLC has the largest legal staff of any of the women's rights legal groups in the country—a commentary on the few legal resources available for this work. The Center's major areas of emphasis are education, employment, income security (including welfare benefits and social security), and women and families—a tall order to cover, but nonetheless, an agenda which still does not include many important issues which warrant attention.

My job, while similar in many ways to the work I did when I first came to the Center in 1972, is now different in many important respects. The administrative tasks are far more substantial. While we are hardly a bureaucracy, the financial and organizational demands are time-consuming. In addition, because the women's rights movement has grown, work with coalitions is far more organized and more of a major part in our efforts. Well-established and on-going working relationships now exist not only with feminist groups such as the National Organization for Women and the National Women's Political Caucus, but also with long-established women's organizations such as the League of Women Voters and the American Association of University Women.

In addition, we and other women's groups work closely with

groups concerned with issues such as civil rights, education, consumer affairs, children, and the elderly. Joint efforts are the rule rather than the exception. Building and maintaining close ties with these groups is a high priority. Our litigation, testimony, and comments are often prepared on behalf of a number of diverse organizations. Meetings on the Hill or with government officials routinely include varied groups with common interests and concerns.

A further new development is the emergence of women in the last few years as a recognized political force. The fact that women perceive that they have particular interests, and see those interests as enhanced or injured by government policies, is now receiving widespread attention. The so-called "gender gap," measuring voting patterns which differ on the basis of sex, has had an enormous impact on our work. Pending legislation affecting women's rights—such as the Women's Economic Equity Act, which addresses a broad range of problems faced by women in areas such as insurance, pensions, and child support—is given high priority by important members of Congress. The Equal Rights Amendment was promptly reintroduced with large numbers of sponsors in both the House of Representatives and the Senate. Attention paid by the press to women's interests has heightened, and Administration officials recognize the implications of women becoming a political force.

I realize now that working in women's rights for so many years has isolated me to some degree from the day-to-day problems many of my colleagues face in dealing with male clients and male bosses who are wary of women lawyers. I have been spared those concerns. However, I have had my share of difficulties in working in a professional setting with men who are unsure about how to treat a woman lawyer—and especially one who works on women's rights. I have served on a number of committees and on boards where I was the only woman, or one of very few. Some men clearly are not yet accustomed to working with women professionals. After getting to know me, it was not uncommon for several to ask my advice about how to treat other women lawyers. They truly wanted to say and do the right thing, but dealing with women as colleagues clearly was not yet a common enough occurrence to come naturally.

Unfortunately, others seemed to be unsure whether any effort was warranted. One lawyer told me his firm was reluctant to hire women lawyers because the firm was afraid that traveling on business trips with a woman lawyer could be uncomfortable and appear improper. Moreover, he said he certainly could not imagine a woman being a partner because a number of his clients would not want a woman handling their accounts.

These comments were made to me quite recently. I can only hope that my responses convinced the lawyer who made them to change his views, and that other lawyers with the same opinions are diminishing in number. It does seem that progress is slow in coming, but then five years earlier, this lawyer most likely would not have even considered the possibility of hiring a woman attorney. One advantage of having worked on women's rights for so long is the perspective I have on the many important gains which women have made since the early seventies.

Although I have been working in this area for 11 years, its appeal remains because of the ever-present challenges and new developments. While none of the basic problems we first began to address in 1972 have been solved by any means, the dimensions and complexities of the issues are better understood. In addition, we have become more aware of the utility of the various law reform techniques developed in the seventies, and we are better able to combine these tools to secure change.

Litigation remains a critical part of our work, but we select our cases with extreme care. We have learned that to be most effective a case must be one piece of a larger strategy, and as such we should be prepared to follow through for an extended period. Quick victories are not only extremely difficult to come by, but often elusive at best.

An example of the evolution of our work—which shows how we stay with a case and bring many other strategies to bear—is in the area of education. One of the first projects I began in 1973 was the development of a lawsuit against the then Department of Health, Education and Welfare (now the suit is against the Department of Education) and the Department of Labor for failure to carry out their obligations to enforce laws prohibiting sex discrimination in schools, including Title IX of the Education Amendments Act of 1972. The suit was filed in 1974 on behalf of six national women's, education, and student organizations and several individuals. It covered elementary, secondary, and most higher education institutions throughout the country. Our case became linked to similar suits alleging failure to enforce laws prohibiting discrimination on the basis of race, national origin, and disability. From the start, the plaintiffs in all of these similar suits and their lawyers worked closely together.

In 1976, we secured a court order requiring broad-based enforcement efforts in some parts of the country; this was expanded in 1977 to include the entire country. The court kept the case open to ensure that the government adhered to its order, and we began to monitor the government's compliance. We later filed several motions with the court seeking still further relief, culminating in a new order issued in 1983. But the government has appealed the decision. Thus, this case, pending for almost 10 years, shows no signs of coming to a close.

In addition to the lawsuit, we have worked closely with a formal coalition of almost 50 Washington-based organizations to monitor agency enforcement of laws prohibiting sex discrimination in schools, to meet with government officials about policies and positions under consideration, and to testify in the House and the Senate on government enforcement. Developments in the lawsuit and the coalition's activities are closely coordinated.

We also determined that, in addition to efforts to secure better government enforcement, it was important to stimulate private enforcement of Title IX. Therefore, we began to participate in precedent-setting cases brought by individuals or organizations directly against schools. We have handled key cases ourselves, and filed friend-of-the-court briefs in cases filed by others.

When we looked to the private bar to bring these cases around the country, it became clear that few lawyers knew anything about sex discrimination laws as they relate to schools. There were no books on the subject and little attention had been paid to the area.

So in 1980, we began work on a text that would analyze both problems of sex discrimination in schools and laws which could be used to challenge those problems. Drafts of that text were used in lawyer training conferences we conducted in six cities around the country over a two-year period. In 1983, we completed the two-volume text, and we have now begun an expanded series of training conferences for lawyers, educators, and school administrators on laws against sex discrimination in schools.

The training conferences have proved to be an important part of our work. Through them, a network has developed around the country of lawyers who are interested in bringing these cases and who are more willing to accept them knowing that the Center is available to help. We also have been able to broaden our understanding about the problems of discrimination in different parts of the country, and about the practical kinds of help we can give to lawyers and educators trying to address them. Each training conference has been a wonderful antidote to the feeling of isolation I sometimes get by working in Washington rather than at the grass roots.

All of the efforts we have undertaken to advance sex equity in schools are painstaking and time-consuming. None will solve the problem overnight. None will work alone.

Our work outside the area of education also reflects a sense of commitment over the long haul. One priority is improvement of child support enforcement. The terribly low amounts of child support paid to women who have custody of children is becoming a national issue. Much work is needed to analyze the effects of pending legislation and to devise strategies to make better use of enforcement mechanisms now in place. Similarly, extensive work is needed as Social Security reforms are proposed to make the system more equitable to women. Our work in the area of employment has also demonstrated the slow pace of progress—and the need for constant vigilance if we are even to remain in place.

The shift in strategy from one of individual cases targeted on specific issues, an approach more common in the early seventies, to the more long-range efforts now in place, presents a tough challenge to the National Women's Law Center. We have been able to grow and expand our staff, but the Center is hardly a permanent institution. In a time of shrinking resources available for such work, NWLC must find a way to secure funding which will place it on firmer footing for the future. That kind of stability is a must if long-range strategies are to be implemented effectively.

The funding challenge, and the continuing need to refine and reassess our priorities and tactics to assure that they are best suited for addressing evolving problems of sex discrimination, are the two most difficult parts of my job. Yet the process of struggling with them, however frustrating at times, keeps us alive and growing.

There are other frustrations, however, which are not as productive. Defeats are particularly painful—not only are my professional efforts at stake (as is true for any lawyer), but the issues are ones about which I care deeply. It is extremely difficult to watch an agency of the federal government not only refuse to move forward, but to reverse hard-won gains secured years before.

Similarly, the internal pressures to take on more work are hard to keep in check. Because clients do not pay for our services, and because the problems are so vast, we are overwhelmed by requests to tackle issues or cases. It is very difficult to refuse to help on an important issue, and none of us are very good at saying no.

To me, however, these frustrations pale next to the rewards. It is a luxury to be able to use my legal training on issues to which I am committed. Moreover, the sense of shared purpose with my colleagues in and outside of the National Women's Law Center has created good friends and strong networks in many areas of the country and in many fields of endeavor. Although some people may no longer work full-time on women's issues, it is rare that they are unwilling to help when possible.

This sense of purpose has been important to me in connection with my daughters as well. Of course, women's rights are important to me because of experiences in my own life. But it is also important that my daughters not find their options limited because of their sex. My older daughter is only now beginning to have any sense of my work, and the meaning of sex discrimination. My younger daughter has no idea of what I really do at all. However, both clearly see and understand that I care about my work, that I believe it is serving an important purpose, and that my husband is proud of what I do. I hope they learn to expect the same for themselves, and are spared the obstacles placed in the way of women of my generation.

CHAPTER 7

AS CORPORATE GENERAL COUNSEL:
Hierarchies With Few Women at Top

BY CATHERINE A. REIN

Myra Alperson

CATHERINE A. REIN

CATHERINE A. REIN

The Continental Group, Inc.
Stamford, Conn.

Education

J.D., New York University Law School, 1968, cum laude; Order of the Coif, Pomeroy Scholar

B.A., Pennsylvania State University, 1964; Class Marshal; Phi Beta Kappa; Evan Pugh Scholar (economics)

Experience

Vice President and General Counsel, The Continental Group, Inc., 1980-present

Vice President and General Counsel, Continental Diversified Operations, (a member of The Continental Group, Inc.), 1978-1980

Secretary, The Continental Group, Inc., 1976-1978

Attorney, The Continental Group, Inc., 1974-1976

Associate, Dewey, Ballantine, Bushby, Palmer & Wood, New York, N.Y., Summer 1967, and August 1968-December 1974

Professional Activities

Admitted to practice in New York, 1968

Member, Corporate Law Departments Committee, 1983-present; Trade Regulation Committee, 1979-1981; Ethics Committee, 1973-1976, Association of the Bar of the City of New York

Member, Connecticut Bar Association

Member, Committee on International Trade, Antitrust Section, 1979-present, American Bar Association

Member, Board of Directors, 1981-present, Bank of New York, Inc.

Member, Board of Directors, 1980-present, Westchester-Fairfield Corporate Counsel Association

Personal

Born: February 7, 1943, Lebanon, Penn.

Married: 1965

Chapter 7

AS CORPORATE GENERAL COUNSEL: HIERARCHIES WITH FEW WOMEN AT TOP

BY CATHERINE A. REIN

Rumor has it that there were only two female general counsel of Fortune 100 companies in 1982. If that is so, it is probably two more than there were in 1979, which I consider encouraging.

I have not yet met the "other" woman but hope that someday our paths will cross to exchange war stories. I have met many other female lawyers who work in corporations and we share many common experiences, but, like our male counterparts, our work life is often very different because of differences in our companies.

How did I end up working for a corporation? Like many other women (and men) who went to law school in the 1960's I did not even know a practicing attorney. My choice of career was built upon the mystique of the Wall Street law firm. I thought that anybody with good grades had to go to a large law firm for the money, but more importantly, for the prestige.

Maybe I should back up a step. I went to a top law school where there were about 20 women in a class of over 300. At the end of the first year, about eight of us were in the top 20 percent of our class. The professors and administration seemed shocked.

Regularly, we were told that this was the best looking class of honor students they ever had, just because they could think of nothing else to say.

The fact of the matter was that the women generally had higher

LSATs and college grades than the men did. Women with lower grades did not aspire to law school in the mid-60's. Actually, no one should have been surprised that we continued to achieve.

Despite our good performance, some of the faculty were not too pleased with the increasing number of women students. An assistant dean told me he disapproved of my getting a scholarship because I would just have children and waste all the effort the school took to train me.

I had heard that song before. In college, I had been told by a student loan officer that there was no money for me because the funds came from industry and industry was not interested in women. He did suggest I switch to education because that was a more acceptable profession for a woman. I must admit, as I look out the window of my office, that I occasionally gloat at proving him wrong.

Of course, all of this was before Title VII of the Civil Rights Act was passed by Congress in 1965. Women have made tremendous career advances since then.

But it wasn't just a new law that helped women lawyers. The war in Vietnam played a large part in our progress. In 1968 when I was job hunting, Wall Street law firms were hiring significant numbers of women for the first time since World War II. This was because their male counterparts were being drafted on graduation. The firms expected the same phenomenon they had seen in the 1940's: Women would work while the men were at war, but then would marry and leave, putting Wall Street back to the *status quo ante.* Only this time it didn't happen that way.

Thus I interviewed for a summer job at the end of my second year and was lucky enough to be hired by a distinguished, old Wall Street firm. Despite my lack of sophistication, I managed to start down what I believe is the best career path for someone who wants to end up as general counsel of a major corporation.

During that summer and the almost six years after law school I spent with that firm, I learned what helping a corporate client was like. In addition, I learned that the legal problems of companies are just as interesting and often more intellectually challenging than the more highly publicized forms of law practice. I even learned that criminal law is part of the daily concerns of corporations; I personally have had to give *Miranda*-type warnings to some high-level executives. I also discovered that practicing law is much more fun than studying law.

Perhaps the most important thing I learned in private practice was to view myself as a professional, with responsibilities and a reputation which belong to me, no matter who my employer might be. This sense of oneself as a lawyer, and the self-confidence which comes with it, are critical in a corporate environment where you frequently have to advise people older and higher in the power structure that what they want to do cannot pass legal muster.

I also learned in private practice how to write and how to analyze legal problems. These skills, I feel, are lost in the law schools' constant search for the "holding" of a case.

As I look back on it now, I almost view my time at the law firm as well-paid graduate school. I enjoyed it, worked very hard, and learned a lot. I am convinced that the experience was critical to the quality of my legal competence today.

So why did I leave Wall Street? Most of life's major decisions cannot be answered in a word and this is no exception.

I had been assigned to represent a small trade association with which a significant client of the firm was affiliated. As counsel to the trade association, I got to do a lot of the day-to-day problem solving that is ordinarily in the domain of in-house counsel. I also got to know my "human" clients personally. I really enjoyed it, and slowly came to recognize that an in-house attorney position would be the most satisfying for me for several reasons.

Practicing law is a great example of a "helping" profession and this is particularly true in the case of in-house counsel. People come to me with problems and I help them solve them. That is a very rewarding way to earn a living.

While outside lawyers may never get to see their clients again, or the long-term effects of their legal advice, inside, you become part of a team and can take continuing pride in your contribution.

And although I still miss many aspects of private practice, especially the sheer stimulation of working in the company of many very brilliant, accomplished lawyers, the sense of belonging to the management team of a large organization which provides products, services, and jobs for millions of people is also a pretty heady feeling.

The nice thing about law as a profession is that you can choose which type of practice is most satisfying to you. Also, you can successfully take on many different types of jobs over the course of a law career. For those who would like to become a corporate general counsel, my advice is: Get in the best law school you can, get the best grades you can, spend three to five years at the best firm you can, work hard on any kind of law which relates to corporations (I was a litigator), and then think about what kind of corporation you want to work for.

First, remember what product the company makes has nothing to do with how interesting your job will be. And, while many law firms require specialization for success, a great advantage to being inside counsel is that you can be a generalist. Most corporations work on the "warm body" approach: if you are the lawyer enroute to the washroom when a problem arrives, it's yours. This results in two things—you are never bored and you are never comfortable that you know all the answers.

I still highly recommend keeping up with one or two relevant areas of the law to maintain some expertise—I was hired as an antitrust expert when I first went to a corporation—but the best job for a company lawyer is general counsel—which means being the chief generalist. After moving in-house, I took on any project I could fit in that no one else wanted to learn about many other areas of law. I eventually moved into a division counsel's job, which resulted in my reviewing my case load one day to discover that I had pending: a customs matter, a Yugoslav joint venture, a worker's compensation claim, two equal employment issues, a Japanese patent license, my departmental budget, preparation for a trip to Europe, and a personnel problem with one of my staff. At that point I decided I had reached my goal and was a true, if harried, generalist.

Getting into a division counsel's position was my second really good career path decision. You learn things about corporate legal issues with plant managers, sales people, and workmen that you never see when your clients are corporate vice presidents, treasurers, and the like. You also come to realize that preventative law is the chief contribution a lawyer can make to his corporate client and to society as a whole. Read any article by or for general counsel, and you will see that avoiding legal problems and holding down legal expenses are top priorities.

When picking a corporation, also remember that you spend many hours at your job, so pick a company with a style and approach you enjoy. I truly believe the difference in most jobs is the people with whom you are working.

When you interview, it should be a two-way street. You should really make an effort to find out what the job content will be, the corporate style, and what opportunities for advancement there are. Ask to talk to both potential peers in the law department and others in the company to whom you will be providing advice.

Once you do make a choice, do not be quick to leave. Advancement takes time. If you are enjoying your job and progressing, hang in there. A resume with too many moves, even upward ones, is hard to explain.

That advice is not always easy to follow. Before I came to my current employer, I had an interview with a national broadcasting company. The work sounded very glamorous and I really liked the associate general counsel. I was called back for a second interview with the general counsel, who kept telling me he did not think I would like the job. I got an offer but was so turned off by the second interview I turned it down.

About six months after I started working, I received a call from the associate general counsel who had just become general counsel. His predecessor had been terminated and he wanted me for the associate's job, which was a better position than I had been seeking and better than the one I was in. I was sorely tempted, but felt it would have been unethical to jump so soon. My career progress to date says I made the right decision—but you never know.

I have been asked many times if it was harder for me to succeed in a corporate environment because I am a woman. My answer is typical of a lawyer: yes and no.

To understand my feelings, focus on the corporate hierarchy and how anyone succeeds in it. Whether you are shooting for the top sales, financial, or legal job, you climb a pyramid with the competition getting tougher in quality and quantity each step of the way. If you do not like to compete, a corporation is not the place for you. It does not have to be vicious, but there is always more than one candidate for each advancement.

Those of us who were used to being rewarded for hard work by good grades often have trouble adjusting to this because unlike A's, the number of promotions is severely limited. Someone is always disappointed.

Women, especially women professionals, have a distinct advantage in this competition while we are still a minority among business managers. Because of our small numbers, we are more visible, and to succeed in a big organization, you must be noticed. Of course, if you screw up, you will probably also get more than your fair share of attention. Yet, I have noticed that it is easier for women to ask questions of male superiors—a good way to avoid mistakes is to find out what your boss wants and what the facts are.

I do believe it is much easier for a woman to get ahead in a corporation if she has a particular expertise, such as law, which is in demand and which everyone in the organization does not believe he already knows more about. In industry, knowledge is power. Through expertise in the law, a young attorney can immediately make a unique contribution to a multi-discipline staff meeting when an equally educated, bright management trainee probably cannot.

I do believe it is harder for a woman to get the very top job in most fields in a corporation. There are many reasons for this: lack of experience, poorly defined career goals, fear of risk-taking, family demands, traditionally all-male corporate team play, others' fear of office romances, and everyday male chauvinism.

We have not yet had as much experience as our male competitors due to our later entry into the fray. Most people believe it takes 20 years of business experience to reach a general manager's job in a Fortune 100 company. That is another reason why law or finance can be a shortcut to success.

Many women, myself included, have not defined career goals as well as men have learned to do. Hence, we frequently skip opportunities for training (such as transfers and lateral moves) which would be steps toward a future goal. This again leaves a woman with gaps in experience which can work against her when a promotion decision is made.

Taking such opportunities sometimes involves risks, which women may find more threatening than do men. When I went to the division counsel's job, I was secretary of our corporation. The transfer was lateral and I had to give up my title and the prestige of dealing with our directors. I spent many a sleepless night deciding whether to make the move. I also was concerned that people would think I had been demoted since I might never again achieve a corporate office. In my case, it was a risk which paid off. People are not always that lucky but successful business people are risk-takers. One thing I have found over and over again is that comfort and success do not go hand in hand.

According to every study I have ever seen, women generally still have primary responsibility for home and family, which takes up time and energy that a male can put into his job. Companies are becoming more sensitive to this problem, but at the top level job, family needs of both men and women are frequently accorded a definite second place. (Ask the successful men you know how many times they have relocated and how their families liked it.) This may not be socially desirable but it is a fact.

When top management decides on which candidate should be promoted, they ask what can each person do well, what skills have they learned, and what experience do they have. They do not ask why one individual has more than another. A woman who takes off several years to have children, or a man or woman who does not acquire certain skills or experience because of an unwillingness to relocate due to family responsibilities, generally will not be the successful candidate.

At lower and even middle management levels, companies will make exceptions for some of these gaps in experience for high potential people. But at the top level, mistakes are too costly and there is no one above to help the inexperienced manager avoid pitfalls.

Expertise, skill, and experience are all critical to success but so are leadership characteristics, and in most companies team play may be the determining factor.

Personality factors are very difficult to measure, and close promotion decisions, even between two qualified male candidates, are frequently made on chemistry.

Top management wants to be comfortable with the members of its team. Older managers are not yet used to working with women, and the unknown always presents a discomfort factor. There is a lot a woman can do to mitigate this issue (and the burden is on her), but it is a problem and will continue to be a negative factor until more women have been in middle and top management jobs for longer.

Mary Cunningham publicity doesn't help either. Corporate executives do not want to leave worried wives at home when they go on business trips. Your only defense against that problem is to get to know the wives so that they can see that you are not a threat. And do not be one. Office romance will hurt your career whether you are married or single, male or female.

I think I ran into most of the traditional male chauvinism I have had to deal with early in my career. This is probably because men were less used to women in the workplace in the 1960's when I started. Because of my youth and inexperience, male chauvinism was hard to deal with at that time, but I learned some lessons which have helped me ever since.

Once, for example, I was scheduled to be the "bag" carrier for a hearing before a state agency. My only role was to hand documents to the senior attorney on the matter. The senior attorney missed the plane.

I met our client at the state capitol. He greeted me warmly and asked where my colleague was. When I told him that I would be handling the matter, his jaw dropped visibly and he turned pale blue.

I immediately assumed he was unhappy with having a female represent him, but there was no time for me to pout or for us to make different arrangements. We attended the hearing and it went very well, especially because the adversary's lawyer was very aggressive and the government officials liked my quieter approach. I noticed my client relaxing and he congratulated me after we left.

On the plane home, I thought the whole thing through and realized his panic had not been male chauvinism but fear that he would have to run the meeting himself. Once he saw I was competent to represent him, the problem evaporated.

Had I been a male, he would have assumed my ability; as a woman I had to prove it. That may be unfair, but I have seen the same sort of response to other women, as well as to myself on subsequent occasions. I have found, in such instances, that proving my competence is all it takes to get past the hurdle and is much more productive than confrontation.

I had another client who was more of a problem. He would offer with great flourishes to take off my coat and carry my bag. At least three times at each conference, he would solicitously ask if I knew where the ladies room was.

I tried my usual "work hard to impress him" routine to no avail. The lesson I learned from this experience was that even I could not win them all. But my batting average is pretty good, and I have still to see a better approach.

Another question frequently asked is whether I have ever experienced sexual harassment. I think that serious harassment of a female lawyer is highly unlikely except by a very stupid or foolish male. First, he should certainly expect us to know our rights. Second, in most companies, lawyers are high enough in the power structure that they cannot be easily threatened with loss of job or promotion for refusing sexual advances. Most corporate executives could not fire a recognized good performer at that level without some credible explanation.

Men aren't the only problem for aspiring female corporate attorneys. Some ask why women do not support each other more in the workplace. I am happy to say this problem is lessening. Mutual support and understanding and the recognition of a responsibility to be a role model are emerging among aspiring women.

I used to say—and believe—I really preferred working with men until an older, wiser woman I knew reminded me that I was writing off more than half of the human race. I soon discovered my preference was only a result of the fact I did not know many other career women. It was not that I did not learn from or enjoy other women on the job. I simply did not know any with common interests and experience. In the corporate world today, this has changed dramatically. Many women are working in lower and middle management jobs now; they are worth looking up because often they have already dealt with problems younger women are facing and they can provide substantial insight or, at least, moral support.

Another issue is the problems of the woman supervisor. I find that managing people, especially lawyers, is the hardest thing I do. My male peers universally agree with me. There is no formula; each subordinate has to be treated as an individual and there are both men and women who for good or bad reasons would prefer a male boss.

One of the reasons is that they believe a male boss has more status and can get more for his people. Another belief is that men are fairer. Still another is that most subordinates want to respect and learn from their supervisors and often women bosses are younger with less experience than members of their staff.

I have found that the best way to deal with any of these problems is to confront them directly and talk with individuals about these attitudes. Respect cannot be demanded, and a good way to earn it is to be honest. A chip on the shoulder or hurt feelings accomplish nothing. So I try to set a goal and get there. If I have to let a male 20 years older than I patronize me a little, I let him if it gets the job done. But if a male/female issue gets in the way, I assert the authority of my position no matter how embarrassing. Managers are judged on results, not popularity.

Also, women managers occasionally fail on people problems. All managers do. This is one of those instances when visibility hurts but it is unavoidable. For example, as general counsel, I regularly preach equal employment opportunity to the other managers in the company. When the legal department was charged with discrimination, I had to swallow hard before entering the next staff meeting. I knew we had not discriminated but I also knew that my inability to avoid the charge would be viewed as a management failure. I took a lot of kidding but could see understanding in the eyes of my peers.

A very current topic today—and one that has caused problems for me—is the two-career couple or family. In a one-career family, the home and personal responsibilities can be delegated to the wife. She buys Christmas presents, waits for the plumber, picks up the children at school and often balances the checkbook.

In a two-career family these and a million other chores must be shared despite two sets of time-consuming job demands. Saturday and Sunday can be eaten up by errands—the drycleaners, post office, shopping and chores—for which there is no time during the week. Often, both spouses are happy to go back to work to relax. My husband and I found that we were often too tired or busy even to talk.

The result is likely to be that each person gets so involved in his or her own life that sharing and romance cannot be sustained. Awareness of the problem should solve it, but does not. While some couples are able to find quiet, fun time together, and to avoid the rut of all work and business-related social commitments, others are not so successful. Many two-career marriages fall apart. My husband and I are still looking for solutions to help us cope with the stress of our professional demands.

Children complicate the problem exponentially, even when families have full-time help. My friends with children often come in to work late or frazzled because the nurse quit, or did not arrive in time from her weekend off.

Society, in my opinion, has not yet found the answer to how women can have both the joys of parenthood and highly successful careers. Every family seems to be a pioneer with more or less success. I do believe that working in a corporation helps. Generally, the demands and hours in a corporate legal job are more predictable than in a law firm. Law, however, is not a 9-to-5 profession for the individual who wants to rise in the corporate hierarchy.

I spent several years as corporate secretary, which meant a regular routine centered around monthly board meetings. My only frantic time revolved around the shareholders' meeting and that, fortunately, was once a year. Then I was promoted to division counsel and was traveling, both domestically and internationally, 40 percent of my time. In between trips, I was trying to get over jet lag and to keep up with the mail that came in when I was out. There was always such a pile that I often felt I was being punished for being unavailable when people wanted me.

After a few months, checks began to bounce, there was no clean laundry at home, and I was getting fat. My husband and I had not faced the changes in our routine; we had not done the necessary rearranging of chores and lifestyle. Fortunately, the frenetic pace ended in a year, but I have colleagues who work this way for years. I admire their stamina and organization but it was not a schedule I would choose.

I did learn that I have to take control of my life and decide priorities because my energy and opportunities are limited. I also learned to accept that I cannot have everything all the time. Priorities have to be reset in the face of change—when a husband or wife is promoted or transferred, when they buy a house, have a child, face a sick parent, or the like.

I find I now use much the same approach at home as I do at work.

I make a list of what I want to accomplish, I set priorities, and then I do one thing at a time. If I focused on all I have to do I would panic, so I take it in manageable pieces. Legal training has helped me here because it tends to cause people to break large situations into smaller components. I have often wondered whether that is because people who like to make lists are attracted to the law or law schools subliminally teach list-making.

But I've also learned that events can sweep aside the list and that doing things on impulse is the spice of life. There is no point being successful if you are bored through routine. Even the most exciting job in the world is still only one dimension of what life offers.

All this is easier for me to say after having succeeded as a corporate general counsel. I believe it took me until I was 30 to learn to have fun. School was hard work. So were my days at the law firm and learning my basic corporate legal skills. I have no desire to go back, to start over again, but I'm still glad to have followed the path I chose. Now I have enough self-confidence to really enjoy my work, and have learned to save time and energy for other pursuits as well.

CHAPTER 8

AS STATE PROSECUTOR: Respected, Abused, Liked, and Hated

BY JANET RENO

Carol Bailey

JANET RENO

JANET RENO

State Attorney's Office
Miami, Fla.

Education

LL.B., Harvard Law School, 1963
A.B., Cornell University, 1960 (chemistry)

Experience

State Attorney, Dade County, Fla., January 1978-present
Partner, Steel Hector & Davis, Miami, 1976-1978
Administrative Assistant State Attorney, Dade County, Fla., 1973-1976
Staff Director, Florida House of Representatives, House Judiciary Committee, 1971-1972
Partner, Lewis & Reno, Miami, 1967-1971
Associate, Brigham & Brigham, Miami, 1963-1967

Professional Activities

Admitted to practice in Florida, 1963
Member, American Bar Association
Member, American Judicature Society
Member, American Law Institute
Member, Florida Prosecuting Attorney's Association
Herbert Harley Award, American Judicature Society, June 1981

Personal

Born: July 21, 1938, Miami, Fla.
Single

Chapter 8

AS STATE PROSECUTOR: RESPECTED, ABUSED, LIKED, AND HATED

BY JANET RENO

In December 1979, Arthur McDuffie, a black insurance man, tried to outrun police on his motorcycle. He was beaten to death. We charged six policemen with crimes ranging from murder to tampering with evidence.

In February 1980, Johnny Jones, a black superintendent of Dade County Public Schools, the fifth largest school system in the country, was charged with grand theft for attempting to use school funds to buy gold-plated plumbing and other fixtures for his personal vacation home.

Jones was convicted in April 1980. Some members of the black community felt I was responsible for the fall of one of the great leaders of the community. Some thought I was racist.

The McDuffie policemen were acquitted in May 1980. Three days of rioting followed. The black community again accused me of being a racist; some demanded I resign.

These events hurt deeply. I felt I had always had a strong commitment to civil rights. Even as a teenager, I had cheered *Brown v. Board of Education.* My response was that the death of Arthur McDuffie had been one of the most horrible events in Miami's history. I felt more strongly about the prosecution in that case than any other matter we had handled. We had committed more manpower, time, and effort to it than we had to any other. If the state attorney could control jury verdicts, the verdict would have been "guilty" but I, of course, could not.

As for Dr. Jones' conviction, I responded that I thought the circumstance surrounding his indictment was a tragedy because the community considered him a leader and a shining role model. However, I said, if we have sufficient evidence to believe that a person committed crimes, we prosecute him, regardless of whether he is black or white or what position he holds. Yes, said some, but you would not have pursued a white public official with vigor. My response was that I would pursue with special vigor any official, black or white, whom I believed guilty of corruption, particularly when it involved our schools.

The dialogue on the conduct of my office continued before groups, committees, commissions, and the media. Other cases were cited. To each I would respond, "Here, review the record. If you think we wrongfully charged someone, tell us why based on the evidence. If you think we didn't do enough, review the record and tell us what we should have done." Only one man asked to review the records or discuss any of the cases.

We subsequently convicted Dr. Jones, in a second case, of solicitation to commit perjury and tampering with a witness. One of his associates was convicted for aiding in the theft of the plumbing. The uproar continued. And I continued to go to the community, to answer questions, and to explain that we had a commitment to try to do what was right based on the law and the evidence.

I refused to resign, saying that to do so, simply to quell an angry mob, would be to encourage anarchy and undermine the democratic, elective process. "Indeed," I reminded those who demanded my resignation in May 1980, "you have a perfect opportunity to get rid of me. I am up for election this fall." No one ran against me. My mother said it was because no one wanted the job.

In the years that have followed since those days in May 1980, I have attempted, consistent with ethical considerations that limit a prosecutor's comments, to explain legal and judicial procedures so our role can be understood. It is a slow process and the "legalese" of my profession has not helped. It is difficult to cut through a lawyer's sometimes stilted language to explain a case without prejudicing the defendant by citing evidence in support of his guilt; to explain why a judge did something without being held in contempt of court; to explain peremptory challenges, immunity, change of venue and other concepts so the public can understand. This has been one of the most difficult and demanding aspects of the job of state prosecutor.

During these years in office, as a focus of community attention, I have had a chance to take stock of myself and my office and to re-examine my feelings toward the law and the judicial system.

I was born in Miami in 1938. Members of my family had worked for both the town's newspapers, in the roles of reporter, photographer, music critic, and copy boy. My parents had come here in the twenties and had grown up with the city. We moved out to the western part of the county, to the country, so we could have cows and horses. I remember backfiring along firebreaks as fires swept through the pinewoods; and milking the cow in the water when the water was so high after a hurricane that we could not find a dry place. I went to public schools here and then to Cornell University and Harvard Law School. I loved Miami: I came home in 1963. A distinguished downtown firm would not give me a job because I was a woman. Fourteen years later that same firm made me a partner.

I worked for a small firm at first, then formed my own two-person law firm, and then, in 1971, went to work for the Florida State Legislature as staff director of the House Judiciary Committee. In my year there, we secured passage of a constitutional amendment reforming the judicial article of Florida's Constitution. That effort introduced me to judges, lawyers, and lawmakers around the state and taught me how laws are made, one of the best things a lawyer and public official can learn. The experience has stood me in good stead ever since.

In 1972, I ran for the State legislature and lost. The next morning I woke up and found a biography of Abraham Lincoln on my bedside table. I started reading and never put it down: Lincoln had lost his first election. In my campaign, I had spoken out on capital punishment and other sensitive issues. The man who was elected Dade County mayor during the same election, had, in the 1950's, cast the lone vote in the Florida Legislature against segregation. He had lost the next election and been down on his luck for a decade—until he became mayor. He had told me, "Janet, do your best; state what you believe. State your position without equivocating. Then, win or lose, you will wake up the next morning feeling good." Later, while in office as state prosecutor, I have constantly remembered those words and have found that I wake up feeling good.

After I lost, the then state attorney surprised me by offering me a job. For the first nine years of my legal career, I swore I would never be a prosecutor because I thought they were more interested in securing convictions than in seeking justice. My predecessor persuaded me to go to work for him, saying I could change that perception. I worked for him for three and a half years. Then I left to go into private practice in the litigation section of a firm representing utilities, banks, and other business interests. I thought I had done enough public service. However, the state attorney resigned in December 1977. Although I urged the Governor to appoint someone else, after a month he asked me to take the job. On January 20, 1978, I was sworn in. The Governor attended the investiture and told the assembled crowd that he had not appointed me because I was a woman; he appointed me because "I stacked up better" than the others. He unwittingly brought down the house with laughter.

I took over an office of 91 lawyers, a total staff of 286, and a budget of $4,480,408. In this office, I am responsible for the prosecution of all crimes and delinquent acts in the Eleventh Judicial Circuit of Florida, which is Dade County. I can file charges by direct information without going to the Grand Jury, except in capital cases. I have subpoena power to compel attendance of witnesses in any investigation.

The basic standard upon which I have operated is that the first objective of a prosecutor should be to make sure innocent people do not get charged. The second objective is to convict the guilty according to due process and fair play. The priorities of the office have consistently been (1) crimes of violence, (2) public corruption, and (3) organized crime, including drug smuggling. While recognizing budget limitations, I have tried to convey that with hard work we can be as good as most law offices, and excellence should be our goal.

After taking office in January of 1978, I faced an election to fill the unexpired term of my predecessor in the fall of that year. I started campaigning immediately, had no Republican opposition, and defeated my primary opponent with 76 percent of the votes cast.

I have tried to be accessible to all who wish to see me. I try to meet with or speak to groups who invite me. I particularly enjoy question and answer sessions. I return all my telephone calls and answer all my mail. At the same time I have tried to adhere scrupulously to the Canons of Ethics and Disciplinary Rules governing a prosecutor's comment and conduct. Thus, the press is regularly told I will not comment on pending investigations. I am called inflexible by some, firm by others and, I am sure, lots of other names behind my back.

Drugs and the illicit dollars and violence associated with them have been one of the major problems of our administration. One of the tensest situations I have faced as a prosecutor involved a drug investigation conducted by our office and local police. We were able to plant a video camera in the office of a drug dealer, and through investigations that followed, we got an unprecedented ringside seat for watching drug smugglers. We infiltrated their activity by my investigators' posing as "bad guys," and using a remote airport as a smuggling operation for planes coming in with drugs. Most federal agencies provided assistance, cooperation, and support. But a few agents claimed we were not doing it right. Three meetings in Washington, D.C. did not eliminate all the federal road blocks. Federal agents threatened my agents with arrest. The media heard of the rumblings and federal documents were leaked to newspaper reporters. We had to persuade the press to hold off, we had to deal with the drug smugglers, and we had to keep the "Feds" happy. We needed then to complete the investigation without alerting the smugglers. The press trusted us enough to give us the time. In the end we charged 120 persons. We were able to arrest 80 of them; most others were outside the country. In the end, all our efforts, including wiretaps, the video camera, and the handling of informants, were approved by the lower court and sustained by the Court of Appeals. But the tremendous time and effort involved in trying to get other agencies to cooperate was frustrating. We had tried to be innovative and adhere to the law, yet federal action discouraged us. Since then, federal cooperation has improved significantly, but the big and bureaucratic federal law enforcement apparatus still seems at times unwieldy.

As Dr. Jones was being convicted in April 1980, scores of Cubans residing in Miami were using every boat they could find which had half a chance to cross the Florida straits to go to Mariel, Cuba and bring back relatives and friends Fidel Castro said he would release. Unknown to us, and to those who risked their lives to bring back those they loved, Castro was snookering us. "If you pick up one family member you must take another person we send you," said Castro's militia as the boats arrived at Mariel. Thus, did Castro dump the dregs of his society from his prisons and his mental hospitals straight into our midst. Miami absorbed over 100,000 Mariel refugees in six months. Most have been law-abiding people who became constructive members of our community. But a relative few, estimated at about 10,000, have been some of the most dangerous, contemptuous criminals with whom we have had to live.

During the summer after Mariel, the crime rate started up dramatically. Through the fall of 1980 and into 1981, Miami reeled under the effects. Fear spread in the face of unprecedented homicide rates. We had to reduce the staffing of all our specialized divisions, including the narcotics division, just to staff the regular felony divisions. During 1980 and 1981, the quality of our narcotics prosecution suffered. While community pressures in this job have not bothered me, the occasional knowledge that we have not handled a major narcotics case as well as we should does. But trying to just keep the system together was our number one objective during the tense days following Mariel and the May riots.

Then Miamians struck back. Law enforcement officials and citizens banded together. Miami Citizens Against Crime, a diverse group of concerned citizens, persuaded the legislature and local city and county commissions to increase my staff and to add more police to the various departments in the county. Crime Watch groups worked together. Citizens volunteered as prosecutors' aides. The spirit was infectious and cut across racial and ethnic lines. Day in and day out I went to meetings of people who wanted to help. My role was to articulate what could be done to combat crime, to stress that there was no simple answer. Longer sentences and more prisons were not the only solutions. I addressed the need for sentencing guidelines, restrictions on parole, more manpower, victim-witness coordination units, early intervention to provide assistance to children headed for trouble, support of our public schools, and increased concern for the family.

With citizen backing, I lobbied the Governor and legislature, explaining why we needed more money for more and better-paid prosecutors. My earlier experience working for the legislature had taught me the "ropes." I knew many of the legislators. With the crime rate being what it was, I did not have to "puff" our needs, and I tried to be as candid and straightforward as I could. Legislators, police, and the citizens trusted us. That is a prosecutor's greatest asset.

In June 1981, the legislature increased our funding by an unprecedented 35 percent. We were able to improve recruiting and training procedures. We now have the resources to respond to crime with sound planning, by reinforcing our strengths and remedying our weaknesses.

From the beginning of my term in office, we had tried to look at statistics objectively to see how the criminal justice system could deal with its many problems more effectively. For example, shortly after I took office, we started to analyze statistics and information relating to homicides to determine how we could better use our resources in this area. We found that a large percentage of homicides involved domestic violence or quarrels between close friends. In response, we established a Domestic Intervention Program staffed by counselors equipped to deal with the knotty problems which lead to domestic violence. We realized that the criminal justice system often did not provide the right alternatives for dealing with the causes of such violence. Jail does not solve the problem of couples who still have some feeling for each other and are trying, though ineptly, to work out their problems. Jail does not solve the problem of a family with financial troubles. The Domestic Intervention Program has worked and has been rated one of the best in the nation. One of my frustrations in office, however, has been my inability to persuade the correctional community to take over and absorb such common sense approaches.

In October 1980, I developed an initial set of plea negotiation guidelines. I wanted to implement guidelines that could be adhered to realistically. I observed them in practice and then expanded them to meet common situations faced by young assistant state attorneys. With respect to felony cases, the guidelines provide that we will not plea bargain unless the bargain produces a good result for the state.

According to the guidelines, prosecutors cannot negotiate a change in sentence without the approval of the victim and arresting officer, unless I or a chief assistant approves. "Do not negotiate armed robberies to less than 10 years, house burglaries to less than 5 years in State prison" are other limits set by the guidelines. We have circulated these guidelines to the judiciary, interested community groups, and others, seeking their comments. We have asked assistant state attorneys to comment on how the guidelines can be improved. They have now been in effect for over a year, and we think they are working. The *Miami Herald* did a study of cases negotiated under the guidelines and reported that we are complying with them. But they also reported that some judges felt we were too inflexible and that we should bear some of the burden of the overloaded judicial system by engaging in more negotiation.

Another key concern of this office has been recruiting young lawyers. In five years, the office has grown from 91 lawyers to 165. At the same time, we have faced the inevitable turnover of young lawyers going to private practice. We recruit from a wide range of law schools and have no stereotyped candidate. Trying to determine what makes a good prosecutor is a fascinating challenge. Young lawyers develop at different paces. Trying to encourage and develop strengths while at the same providing firm guidelines for conduct without stifling young lawyers is a delicate issue we face day in and day out. With experience, we are getting better at the task.

Not all of our time has been spent dealing with murderers, public corruption, drugs, and planning. In January 1982, a new character came into our lives and added a different dimension to prosecution. Prince Turki, then fifth in line to the throne of Saudi Arabia, came to Miami to reside with servants, wealth, and ritual that was unusual even for this city. After he had been here awhile, we received complaints that his servants were being mistreated. We attempted to check these allegations through the prince's representatives and met a stone wall. After contacting Washington to make sure the prince did not enjoy diplomatic immunity, we attempted to serve a search warrant, but were met by resistance from the prince's bodyguards and even the princess herself. The prince sued my chief assistant. The State Department started calling, and an unofficial ambassador was eventually sent to town to tell us the prince was important to our government and the oil supply might be cut off if we prosecuted him. That was my first exposure to the State Department and the arcane ways of international diplomacy. The State Department expressed the hope that I would not prosecute the prince and princess. I explained that they had resisted the officers and, unless someone offered proof of their innocence, I had more than sufficient evidence to charge them. Again, high ranking officials explained the delicate nature of relations with Saudi Arabia. "Why," we said, "should a prince and princess be treated any differently than an American citizen who would certainly have been charged under the circumstances?" When we persisted in prosecuting, the State Department suddenly conferred diplomatic immunity on the prince and his family. Shortly thereafter they left the country. Recently, I received a report from a person who had been working in Saudi Arabia. A government official there wanted to know about "Judge Reno," who had forced one of the high ranking members of the royal family to leave the United States. My reporter said that the Saudis were not as upset by the fact that he had been forced out, as by the fact that a woman had done it.

What have I learned as state prosecutor?

I have learned that the law is not always right. The law is not always what it should be. To attempt to weave the law in a fair fashion through the human tragedies, emotions, and conflicts of a great and growing city that has become the nation's melting pot—to achieve justice in the end—is what this job has been about.

I have also learned that my office is the common denominator of the criminal justice system in a jurisdiction of 26 different police agencies. I think it is our responsibility to look through the violence, gore, and fraud they deal with to understand why people commit crime; to look beyond the criminal justice system to other institutions that may have failed the criminal to see what can be done to prevent crime and to make the system better. We have tried to speak out on behalf of the entire jurisdiction, to challenge ourselves and the system.

What effect has my being a woman had? None, I would say. About five months after I took office, a newscaster for a local television station said that when I was sworn in, he felt so bad for me because he did not think a woman could do the job. Five months later he said he had changed his mind. I think I am respected, abused, liked, and hated in my role as a prosecutor, as a person, not as a woman. At the same time I have been personally treated with gentle courtesy by most men, including police officers, black leaders, and Hispanic merchants who do not seem troubled at all by the fact that they are dealing with a woman.

Miami is emerging as the most exciting city in the Western Hemisphere. It has become an international banking center, a market for Latin America, a medical center for the area, and a crossroads for transportation. It has become one of America's most international cities. But the growing pains are still here.

On December 28, 1982, a young black man was shot to death by a police officer. Disturbances erupted once more. While the community went forward to an Orange Bowl Parade and New Year's game without incident, the focus turned once again on me and how I would handle this shooting. I would again try to do my best to do what is right based on the facts and the law.

In the midst of tensions, I will remember the meeting of the young black prosecutor who during those December disturbances saved the life of a Cuban lady who spoke no English. He braved an angry brick- and bottle-throwing mob to pull her from her car, which had been halted by the mob, and he got her to safety. Others took her to the hospital. She had not known his name and had not been able to thank him. So she came to my office to meet him. When she saw him, she threw herself in his arms sobbing her thanks. He held her and comforted her with a few words of Spanish. That is the Miami I love. That is what makes this job worthwhile.

CHAPTER 9

AS FEDERAL PROSECUTOR: Talking Man-to-Man

BY JO ANN HARRIS

Myra Alperson

JO ANN HARRIS

JO ANN HARRIS

Private Practitioner
New York, N.Y.

Education

J.D., New York University of Law, 1972, cum laude; Editor, New York University Law Review, 1970-72; Order of the Coif; NYU Founder's Day Award, 1972; Benjamin F. Butler Memorial Prize, 1972; Edmond Cahn Law Review Award, 1972; Pomeroy Scholar

B.A., State University of Iowa, 1955 (magazine journalism)

Experience

Private Practitioner and Of Counsel to Schulte, Roth & Zabel, 1983-present

Executive Assistant United States Attorney, United States Attorney's Office, Southern District of New York, 1983

Senior Litigation Counsel, United States Attorney's Office, Southern District of New York, 1981-1982

Chief, Fraud Section, Criminal Division, Department of Justice, 1979-1981

Deputy Chief, Criminal Division, United States Attorney's Office, Southern District of New York, 1978-1979

Assistant United States Attorney, Criminal Division, United States Attorney's Office, Southern District of New York, 1974-1978

Law Clerk, Lawrence W. Pierce, United States District Judge, Southern District of New York, 1972-1974

Publishing Career, Time Incorporated (1960-1969); Meredith Publishing Company (*Better Homes and Gardens,* 1956-1960); Curtis Publishing Company (*Ladies Home Journal,* 1955-1956)

Professional Activities

Admitted to practice in New York, 1973

Member, Criminal Law Section, Litigation Section, American Bar Association

Member, Association of the Bar of the City of New York (Council on Criminal Justice; Corrections Committee)

Member, National Institute for Trial Advocacy (NITA) teaching team for

National Program, June 1980, July 1981, June 1982, July 1983; teaching team for Northeast Regional, August 1978, August 1982

Team Leader, NITA Northeast Regional, August 1979

Member, Law School Advocacy Programs teaching teams (Harvard University Law School, fall 1977, 1978, 1982, 1983, and winter 1981; Hofstra University Law School, winter 1978, 1979, 1980, 1981; Emory Law School, winter 1982; team leader, winter 1983

Graduate, Program for Senior Managers in Government, John F. Kennedy School of Government, Harvard University, August 1980

Personal

Born: May 18, 1933, Macomb, Ill.

Married: 1965

Children: Two stepchildren, two grandchildren

Chapter 9

AS FEDERAL PROSECUTOR: TALKING MAN-TO-MAN

BY JO ANN HARRIS

I am 5'11" tall, and have a low-pitched voice which, when projected, can break a brick at 50 yards.

Of all the qualities born and bred which have contributed to whatever success the law has brought me, in the courtroom and in the office, I credit these two factors most. I don't mean to discount what is probably more than a modest ability to think and write, or the legal education and experience which honed it; nor can I dismiss out of hand my compulsive Type A behavior, shared with all crazy people in this business; and, lord knows it is not my intention to discourage shorter women with thinner voices. But, the plain fact is that these attributes—casually dealt by forces wholly out of my control—are priceless in a trade which places a premium on command presence. They are intimidating. They mean I can walk into a courtroom and automatically get the attention I need to conduct the trial of a case, and more importantly, they permit me to be my naturally low-key self without doing great harm to my cause. I have never raised my voice emotionally in a courtroom at opposing counsel, the jury, or the judge. I could not. It is not my style and would ring false. Fortunately I need not, because I can whisper with this voice and be heard by the audience I want to reach. I have come to know and finally rely on the probability that however terror-stricken I may be about, for instance, what a witness is going to say, or worse yet, what I am going to say, most people will see a 5'11" woman lawyer with an assured voice apparently in total command of the situation, or at least, of herself.

The advantage is incalculable.

I did not always feel this way. For the first 40 years of my life—until I tried my first case—I regarded the height as a burden to be borne and the voice as a distinct liability. Towering over peers both female and male, and being mistaken on the telephone, more often than not, as the latter, was not the image I would have chosen.

Maybe that's why I turned to pen and paper for expression as early as grade school and followed that interest into a degree in magazine journalism from the State University of Iowa in 1955, and a career with a series of major publishing companies which eventually took me to Time Inc. in New York in 1960, where I happily labored until 1969. Then one morning for the first—and only time in my life—I talked with the proverbial mirror. The conversation was short and decisive. Within two months I took the LSATs, and the following fall of 1969 the first-year class at New York University Law School included a 36-year-old woman who never, but never, talked in class. Three years later I graduated with a J.D., adorned with highest honors all premised on a certain skill with the written word. I still had not talked—voluntarily, at least—in class and, indeed, had become considerably adept at subverting the Socratic method.

From NYU I went directly to a judicial clerkship with a United States District Judge in the Southern District of New York. Still I had not raised my voice, until one day in mid-trial sometime in 1974. I was with the judge in one of the large ceremonial courtrooms which grace our courthouse. The court clerk, who usually administered the oath to witnesses, was not on hand. A witness ended his testimony. The next was called. Still no court clerk. "Swear the witness," the judge whispered. There was no way out. With heart thumping, I dutifully took up the oath and commenced to lead the witness through the ritual. "Louder," hissed the judge. And louder I did it. The voice I had always hidden filled that courtroom. And it was sonorous, and vibrant, and full of authority, without being overbearing. It was wondrous. I suspect that little moment changed my life. It is not just that a future as a trial lawyer may have jelled then and there; it's that in being a trial lawyer, I have grown in countless ways over the last 10 years.

There is, in my view, nothing that so powerfully focuses the mind as trying a case. Indeed, although I recognize that reasonable people differ (and, perhaps, only unreasonable people agree), it is a complete way of life. To me, a case is a box circumscribed on all sides with facts to be reconstructed and then communicated to a group of ordinary people—jurors—who are in the middle of one of the most intense times of their lives. A case has a beginning, a middle, and an end. It is played with rules which, alone, are fascinating puzzles to be solved and applied. A case binds people together in ways which must be similar to soldiering under incredible pressure. It brings out the best and worst in people. It is, in a sense, war—simplifying, streamlining, enhancing every waking moment (and, on trial, there are a multitude of waking moments). The case itself may be petty, but the process is all consuming. It pushes the less precise concerns of life to the side. I go on the wagon for every trial, for two reasons. The first is that I need to have virtually every sense operating at full capacity. But further, trying a case is itself an incredible "high."

How have I grown? I have gained a vast knowledge about other people's areas of expertise. The profession, of course, offers that opportunity to every practicing lawyer, but my specialty compels me not only to learn the field surrounding a case, but to communicate it, not just to other lawyers and judges, but to people from all walks of life for whom I have enormous respect—petit jurors. This challenge forces far greater concentration and produces far greater satisfaction. Thus, I have learned about dozens of specialized fields from securities and commodities, to paper manufacturing and medicine, because at some time or another I had to know more than anyone else in a courtroom on the subject.

But beyond such extrinsic knowledge, through some process I don't fully understand, I have come to know me, and to rest a good deal of quiet confidence in me, not only in court, but everywhere. Perhaps it is because in trial work you so frequently put yourself on the line—and win or lose, get up, no matter what, and try again. Perhaps it's because in my line of work, you see so many tragically broken lives. Perhaps it's because you learn, in prosecuting cases, to mold and lead a team of people with diverse professional talents and human problems. Whatever it is, I feel I am pretty much what I always hoped to be: a decent, reasonably bright person, with a well-developed sense of responsibility; an ability to make decisions; a healthy skepticism, fairly well-tempered with a dose of compassion; a record that shows I won't necessarily screw up in court; and, finally, the ability to laugh, or at least chuckle, at my own mistakes.

Now, how did I reach this state and are there meaningful messages in this for other women?

The reason I shifted from publishing to law is lost to historic revisionism, if I ever really knew it. The fact is that the decision came first, without apparent forethought; the reasons developed later as a result of persistent questioning by astonished friends and, later, curious journalists. I love publishing, and thoroughly enjoyed my 14 years working in the field. Ink still courses through my veins; I still own my own printing press and several fonts of type. I married a journalist in 1965 and, with him, still follow the business avidly. There was virtually nothing in my life—except a fascination with facts and the way things work, and a keen competitive sense—which might have signaled a change in careers to the law.[1]

Certainly at the time I made my decision, I didn't believe it was remotely based on a sense of frustration or even the conscious idea that my career was stuck because I was a woman.[2] Nor, in my

1. Time Inc. was a wonderful place to work. Although it was beyond the stage of the Fun House described by William Brinkley, it was still a wacky corporation which treasured its talented nuts, and was, I thought, secretly run by a group of rummy old ladies who had kept the place going during the big war. In any event, the company had been exceedingly good to me. They sent me to London to live and work for awhile, and the job facilitated most of the world-traveling I've done.

2. If I had been more sensitive, I suppose I would have gotten mad or depressed in 1963 when my liberal boss bemoaned, generally, the fact that I didn't have "balls" (he was referring to a physical, not a mental, characteristic) when the powers-that-were promoted someone other than me to a job I would just as soon not have had. What he said, I now recognize, is actionable, but even if I had been sensitized then, I don't think I would have sued him, or the company. It's just not in me, to this day, to cause that sort of personal fuss. I much prefer fighting over someone else's turf, and, indeed, probably have a reputation for never getting emotionally involved in a case, any case. Besides, the man had already put me in a position where I was supervising a small staff of men writers and artists, and had put himself on the limb by insisting that my job entitled me to attend meetings in remote beach resorts where, for years, I was the only woman among 50 hard-drinking, poker-playing men.

ignorance, did I give any thought to problems I might encounter on that ground in the law. I talked with the man who was then chief counsel at Time Inc. He was unflagging in his support and enthusiasm for my decision, and never mentioned the possibility of bias. I talked with women practitioners, not because they were women, but because they were the only other lawyers I knew. Those conversations focused on my great concern about getting into law school and managing the work load at my advanced years; it never crossed my mind that there were other possible barriers beyond the limits of my own capacities.[3]

Thus, I joined the mass of people who poured into law schools in the late 1960's and discovered that, despite the 15-year age spread, I was motivated by the same events—the drive for civil rights, the real concern about the Vietnam War,[4] a feeling (which I now recognize was overblown) that lawyers were in control of everything.

For me, three important career-shaping phenomena happened in law school. First, I found that not only could I do the work, but I thrived on it. It opened up a whole new world and a whole new way of thinking about that world. The corporate structure at Time Inc. was downright bohemian and anarchistic compared with the legal process. True, the legal process needs a bit of enlivening, which I have always tried to provide in my practice. But it is logical, rational, sensible. I had, for more years than I like to remember, regarded myself as creative, unbound—yet I went for this disciplined process like a duck to water.

The second event was my decision that the world I wanted to change, or at least actively participate in, was the criminal justice system. I can remember applying for a position in NYU's trend-setting Criminal Law Clinic for my third year and thinking I'd lost it when I candidly disclosed my intention to become a prosecutor

3. I know this sounds hopelessly naive, and there's no accounting for it in my background, except to note that my truck driving father and office-clerking mother worked long hours to assist my brother and me to become the first to go to college from our long line of midwestern farmers. I guess in their work, questions of gender bias had simply never risen, and a college degree was a ticket to anything.

4. My husband had covered the Vietnam War for NBC Television News in the late 1960's, and I had worked in Hong Kong, on leave from Time Inc., to be near him. But that's a different story.

because, in my view, that was where the power to do justice rested, not with the defense bar. But I got one of the slots, declining an offer to become an executive on the law review to hold it. Indeed, I cleaned up my third-year responsibilities on the law review within weeks in order to throw myself into the clinic's defensive practice of criminal law. That year on the defense side absolutely convinced me that I was right—my natural concerns for fairness in the system would be far better exercised on the other side. Besides, there could be little doubt that prosecutors—as lawyers—simply had the better job because they bore the burden of proof and, thus, had all the fascination of piecing together the facts. It really didn't occur to me until much later, when I was exercising this power, that in addition to all of this, responsible prosecutors have a far simpler ethical road to travel. My client has *always* been served when I do the right thing, even if it means dismissing or losing a case. Indeed, one of the major satisfactions of the various roles I have played in the Department of Justice has come from the responsibility to use this power in the public interest up to its very limits, and *no further;* to exercise it in decisions not to prosecute as firmly as in decisions to indict. It is easy to get up and go to work every day to a job that not only permits that sort of righteousness, but demands it.

A choice of career track was the third important event. Although a good many years and life experiences separated me from most of my law school colleagues, my general attitude was that we were all at year one when it came to the law, the consuming focus of all our lives. It was, of course, a concession forced upon me by circumstances, but it not only resulted in a good many younger friends, it also led inevitably to my decision to attempt a career track commensurate with my "legal" age, instead of my chronological years.[5]

---

5. I have never regretted the decision, although it has had certain definite consequences. Between my second and third years at NYU I did the usual summer at one of the city's major law firms and later that year was pleased to get an offer from them. I liked the people a lot (there was something about the atmosphere that was reminiscent of the best of Time Inc.), but for once I noticed the lack of women in the middle, not to mention the top. I mentioned this along with my far more pressing concern—age discrimination. I got assurances on the gender question which I believed. They said they had two classes of women. Those who had been around forever and who had come to the firm with the understanding that no

Thus, with many of my friends, I entered the fray for a judicial clerkship with every hope of moving from that job to a federal prosecutor's job in the best public law office in the country—the United States Attorney's Office for the Southern District of New York. (Never mind that I would later find myself a 41-year-old among the 26-year-olds in the Southern District Criminal Division's Short-Trials Unit). Fortunately, moving toward graduation, I found a judge who could not have cared less that I was almost as old as he (and taller).[6] And no one bothered to tell me that historically the United States Attorney's Office in the Southern District of New York was infamous for its view that women weren't tough enough to prosecute. Indeed, nothing in my brief legal history at that time had quite prepared me for such an outlandish idea.[7]

---

partnership was in the offering, and the recent wave of young associates, forged in the 1960's, who were very much in the running. I was in the latter group, they said, and I believe that had I accepted the offer then, that's where I'd be now, rolling in money, and probably enjoying myself, unaware of how much I'd missed. They were candid about my age concern and told me that 40 was more than a personal benchmark, that it would probably be a professional watershed, and that if I, at 39, did not instantly move under the protection of some large private law firm, I'd find myself frozen out of that particular kind of institution.

This advice rang true, comporting with my view of American business, which does not like to invest in people who have what appears to be less than 40 productive years ahead of them; so it was with eyes wide open that I exercised my option to continue on a track designed for people with all the time in the world. I know now that in so doing I may have closed a door. As a result, I am not rich. And to enter the private practice of law now, I cannot look to the relatively riskless world of the large law firm without a very special situation.

6. The year was 1972, when the number of women law clerks among the total of 58 in the Southern District of New York doubled. My judge distinguished himself by claiming two of the ten. He was, indeed, the first in that court to fill his complement with two women. My co-clerk (5'10"; quiet voice which, projected, could break, at the least, glass) has since followed me to the Criminal Division of the United States Attorney's Office, as have two more of the judge's women law clerks. (Neither of the latter tops 5'2".) The four of us constitute some sort of a record for a single judge, and that says a lot about the quiet, confident strength of the man and the wonderful quality of the experience he provided.

7. I had left Time Inc. blissfully unaware that part of the reason may have been discrimination—and I still doubt that it was instrumental. The law school I chose to attend fielded a class which was fully one-third women, who—now that I think about it—probably performed at a level disproportionate to our numbers. Women

It is probably not surprising then that when I interviewed with the United States Attorney's Office, I was, again, more concerned about age discrimination than gender problems. It had not totally escaped my notice that there were only two women among the approximately 80 prosecutors in the office, but I simply would not believe they could ignore my very vocal (but quiet) insistence that I hadn't gone that far to be put in the Civil Division. They didn't. Instead they ignored the fact that I was a woman. The matter was resolved, I think, when I was ushered into the sitting room of a male chauvinist terror-of-the-office, who started the interview with the memorable: "Now, let's talk this out man-to-man." For the sake of my more sensitive sisters in this business, I wish I could say that I properly slammed him in his place. The fact is that I burst out laughing. I simply couldn't take seriously the implication of what he was saying, and proceeded to talk with him the way I talk with everyone, which is pretty straightforward in any event.

I was hired for the Criminal Division with a class that was otherwise all male, among whom I still count some of my closest professional friends. Within two years, the office started hiring vast numbers of women as prosecutors, most of them, incidentally, ranging from 5'1" to 5'5", and it is crystal clear now that women suffer utterly no disabilities as prosecutors. The notion that in women tough-mindedness and effectiveness have to translate into bitchiness or some other non-feminine form of behavior has simply been laid to rest here. This is not to say that we don't have a few obnoxious people, male and female. But the special quality of this office has always been its collegiality. Indeed, we are extraordinarily close to each other precisely because the rest of our professional world is

---

professors were few and far between, but it never dawned on me that this was the result of any bias. In truth it never dawned on me at all. One woman professor was exceedingly helpful to me, but I believed at the time—and still do—that she was acting as a lawyer toward a person she perceived to have more than a modest potential as a lawyer. At least I recall no woman-to-woman chats. She simply whaled into my writing style and forced a modicum of discipline upon me, and then got me a paying legal job between my first and second years, no easy task. I look back now and admire her for what she must have put up with during her legal career, and recognize that part of her pride in me now is special because I am a woman—but I daresay, she might deny it.

arrayed against us. This special atmosphere instantly absorbed me and every one of the dozens of women who followed me, without dropping a beat. No favors; no slights; no quarter. The judges, by the time we started appearing before them in all our numbers, had very nearly all had women clerks, or had learned to bury any negative feelings.

There are still times, even today, when a judge takes the bench and says without thinking—or looking— "good morning gentlemen."[8] I don't tend to hold such presuppositions against them as long as they don't take it out on my case. My basic attitude about such judges: bemusement. I'm not about to risk a case for the sake of a bit of personal therapeutic ventilation.

I am, indeed, very slow to anger on this subject, but there are limits. In 1979, I went to Washington in *Newsweek*'s words, "as the first woman to head a major prosecution section of the Justice Department." The Fraud Section at the Department in Washington at that time numbered about 67 lawyers, 85 percent male. I took the job for reasons that anyone would understand: professional ambition and personal growth. Although I stood to gain much from the ex-

---

8. It's a little harder to take when they say "good evening, gentlemen" when you've been trying a case before them all day, not to mention weeks, which is what a judge in one of my trials did from time to time. I bided my time, although it was beginning to get under my skin. At the end of one day when all of the attorneys and a fine woman legal assistant on our team were in the robing room, he finally caught himself. From the trial transcript:

THE COURT: Anything else? All right, you gentlemen are done now. I have to do some work. See you in the morning. And ladies.

MS. HARRIS: Thank you, your Honor.

The transcript, of course, doesn't reflect the inflection, but the response was delivered with reasonably good humor. This particular judge was, in most respects, more than lawyers on either side could hope for in the trial of a criminal case—hardworking, informed, patient, attentive, fair. Those attributes far outweighed his tendency to ignore my presence as a woman, which I attribute to habit, not intent. Besides, this was the same judge who months before, when I had entered the case, had said to assembled male counsel:

THE COURT: I should warn defense counsel Ms. Harris is, if not the best prosecutor I have ever seen, certainly one of the best.

Now, how can you hold an occasional slip of the tongue against a man who has not only boosted your ego like that, but in the process helped psych the other side in pretrial maneuvering for position?

perience, it was not without personal cost. With my husband's support, I was undertaking not only a major job but a commuting marriage. With considerable shock on the day I reported to work I learned that "the entire Section was in open revolt over my appointment." Somehow the men (and women) lawyers in the Section had gotten the idea that I was a choice dictated by affirmative action. Now that was a new experience for me, to say the least. I was appalled, angered, and, yes, humiliated. I took a walk directly to the Supreme Court to hear the argument in a case tried by a close friend of mine in New York, collected my thoughts, remembered that my mother preached that hard work and talent win out, and finally marched to Section headquarters to meet the troops.

My saintly mother was right. I never mentioned what I regarded as a gross insult, but instead simply rolled up my sleeves and went to work. It was a wonderful two years, full of professional respect and personal friendship. So far as I know, not one of those men (or women) ever harbored a problem reporting to me, or working with me. The reason was really pretty simple. I was myself, and I am pretty good at what trial lawyers do. They were trial lawyers. I am also traditional enough to understand, I think, the problems men have managing less traditional women, and I took great care not to undermine the men managers working for me when I felt they'd done an injustice, or given special favor, to women working under them. The imbalance was corrected, not by me, but by the men, after an occasional quiet, private session with me.

In retrospect, I learned a vast amount about people and myself during my Washington experience. I found that I was comfortable managing people, and was reasonably good at it. But, in addition, the job compelled me to expand my outside-of-the-office professional activities. The cabin fever resulting from that desk-bound position drove me to accept invitations to speak and participate on panels before bar associations and law schools around the country. Prior to that time, I had ducked such invitations because I frankly find it hard to listen to, let alone speak on, policy matters with a straight face. They are mushy subjects. Such things are better left to politicians. I am a strictly meat-and-potatoes facts person, and am more than a little embarrassed to solemnly pronounce anything, let alone yet another "war on white-collar crime," when I know the facts simply don't support the rhetoric. So I didn't pontificate. But, it turned out that my down-to-earth, plain-talking style seemed to communicate with and, indeed at times, outrage an audience. As I gained the confidence to do that, I found these appearances, although they were no substitute for a case, at least stimulating and fun.

More important to me, the sedentary nature of the Justice Department job propelled me to expand my outside teaching activities to keep my own skills from atrophying. Since 1977, I had taught at a number of trial advocacy programs for a variety of law schools and the National Institute for Trial Advocacy. I did so because I have a deep commitment to the training of young lawyers, including young women lawyers who attend in droves, but also because I found the experience almost as exhilarating as trying cases. Next to handling a case myself, there is nothing quite like watching terrified young lawyers develop the skills and the confidence to do it themselves after a week or two of intense tutelage.

Between the Washington-based speaking and teaching, I got a broader exposure to lawyers from around the country. The experience dragged me out of what I now realize is the idyllic seclusion of a prosecutor in the Southern District of New York, where women simply do the job and are recognized accordingly, and where I have never seen fear or favor operate because the prosecutor is a woman. Judges, defense attorneys, agents, witnesses, and even defendants are too wrapped up in the pressure of the case to pay a whole lot of attention to the gender of the person wielding the prosecutor's power.[9]

But, as I traveled around the country working with experienced trial lawyers (mostly men) and young lawyers (a healthy mixture of men and women), I learned about the problems of men and women in this profession, and now reluctantly accept the proposition that the tenet of my background is not necessarily cast in stone. It may very well be that the power which resides in a prosecutor's office has protected me and my colleagues from grosser forms of sex discrimi-

9. Certainly defendants adjust quickly. I am reminded of a call I got last year after I was assigned to try a major tax fraud case. It was from a man I had convicted several years ago. He had finished his four years up-the-river and simply called to wish me luck and to express his sympathy for the defendant.

nation not easily overcome by hard work and competence. I hear horror stories from young women law students and lawyers working their way up the big-firm ladder. I compare them with women in our office out of school the same number of years, with essentially the same backgrounds, who are accomplished, responsible lawyers and people—open, hard working, confident. The difference is shocking. In my judgment, it can only be attributed to the reality that we have been nurtured in an atmosphere which has required us to spend virtually none of our energies and resources fighting the gender battle.

However, we are now at the threshold of interesting times on this subject. The large number of women who came to this office in the 1970's from clerkships and two year stints at law firms have now completed their four year commitments. If the "old boy network," in fact, has become merely "the old network," these women should be moving out and taking their well-earned places at the private bar. They aren't, yet, in normal numbers. I recognize that times are bad for law firms, and perhaps that's the reason. But I am not at all amused by the messages I hear from the private bar. Most men will concede that there is a belief that women can't bring in business; and most honest men will admit that, in fact, it's an excuse which covers a multitude of sins, most involving preservation of assorted, comfortable "old boy" arrangements.

This attitude strikes me as silly, as did the need—so many years ago—to talk with me "man-to-man," in order simply to talk straight. Except this time, no one is bursting out laughing. If the private bar doesn't adjust quickly, elephantine law firms, already vulnerable because of their size and consequent fee structures, may find—not lawsuits (who has the time for that?)—but some fierce competition from lean, mean small firms formed by people (women and men) who have grown up and gotten very good at what they do together in an atmosphere that values talent and collegiality, period.

With this, my not-so-saintly father-in-law's motto comes to mind: "Don't get mad; get even."

Editor's Note: Since writing this chapter, Jo Ann Harris has launched her own private law practice. She is also Of Counsel to New York's Schulte, Roth & Zabel, where her office is located.

CHAPTER 10

AS GOVERNMENT OFFICIAL: Being a Woman Pays Off

BY ANNE P. JONES

Julie Wiatt

ANNE P. JONES

ANNE P. JONES

Sutherland, Asbill & Brennan
Washington, D.C.

Education

LL.B., Boston College Law School, 1961; Order of the Coif, Boston College Law Review

B.S., Boston College, 1958 (Social Sciences)

Experience

Partner, Sutherland, Asbill & Brennan, Washington, D.C., September 1983-present

Commissioner, Federal Communications Commission, March 1979-June 1983

General Counsel, Federal Home Loan Bank Board, 1978-1979

Director, Division of Investment Management, Securities and Exchange Commission, January 1976-January 1978

Associate Director, Division of Investment Management, SEC, August 1972-January 1976

Legal Assistant to Commissioner James J. Needham, SEC, July 1970-July 1972

Special Counsel, Division of Corporate Regulation, SEC, April 1969-July 1970

Attorney Advisor, SEC, April 1968-April 1969

Associate, Ropes & Gray, Boston, Mass., 1961-1968

Professional Activities

Admitted to practice in Massachusetts, 1961

Member, Federal Bar Association (Securities Law Committee and Savings Institutions Law Committee)

Member, American Bar Association (Federal Regulation of Securities Committee)

Member, American Law Institute

Member, Massachusetts Bar Association

Member, Board of Trustees of Boston College (Executive Committee)

Personal

Born: February 9, 1935, Arlington, Mass.
Married: 1981

Chapter 10

AS GOVERNMENT OFFICIAL: BEING A WOMAN PAYS OFF

BY ANNE P. JONES

By actual count I graduated from law school about 22 years ago, in June 1961. Judged from the perspective of a woman lawyer, so many changes have taken place since then, that my graduation seems a century ago.

To begin with, there was only one other female in the law school class of 1961. Both of us were law review members and clearly in the top 10 percent of our class. I believe that both of us enjoyed law school, but still suffered the slings and arrows of outraged male students who were convinced we were occupying places which rightfully should have gone to men. Clearly neither of us (in their judgment) would ever practice law, but rather would marry and gracefully (or otherwise) retire from the profession.

Despite being female, I had relatively little trouble finding a clerkship the summer between my second and third years at school. I had finished first in the class the first year, and a fair number of large firms in Boston indicated an interest in employing me. My recollection of that summer is very favorable. I was assigned a number of different research projects, covering, as I recall, a wide range of subjects from trusts and estates (a spendthrift trust question) to corporate law (a stock dilution question). It was a somewhat intimidating, but on the whole a very pleasant and rewarding experience, which in no way prepared me for my third year and the challenge of seeking a permanent job.

I had, by the way, retained my number one class standing after exams in the second year, but I returned to law school to find the first of the many sexist discriminations which plagued all women in those days. Precedent had established that the student with the highest rank at the end of the second year would be editor-in-chief of the law review. (Actually this was not a long-held precedent because the law review was then of fairly recent vintage.) However, never before had a female been in that position. The subject was never overtly raised, but the managing editorship went to the gentleman who was second in the class both the first and second year, and various minor editorships went to the gentlemen who were third, fourth, fifth, and so on. I guess my female colleague and I were lucky to be able to write comments and have them published!

Then the time arrived to see what law school had prepared us for, and consistent with the practice in those days, we all went looking for that first, seemingly very important, association. I received an offer from the U.S. Department of Justice, Attorney General's Honor Program, to work in the Antitrust Division, as well as one from the National Labor Relations Board. At the time, however, I was interested in remaining in the Boston area and, based on my summer experience the year before, thought I wanted to try my hand at private practice. In those days, as I recall, no firms came to the school to interview, so phone calls to set up appointments and trips to the city to meet the managing or hiring partner of as wide a variety of firms as possible occupied the time of most third-year students. For some reason (could it be merit!), I had no difficulty convincing the appropriate partners that they should see me, so I was almost totally unprepared for the reception I received at a large number of the prominent Boston firms. I had decided to confine my search to the top 10 or so (by size and reputation). While I made no attempt to keep track of the number of interviews I had or the rejections, I believe I received offers from only two. At one of the rejecting firms, I was literally told that I would have no trouble finding a job because I had done so well in law school, but that they simply did not hire women. At least two of the rejecting firms asked if the fact that I attended a Catholic institution was indicative of my being Catholic. The managing partner of one of those firms then opined that since I am Catholic, I did not believe in birth control and that, therefore,

I would have children, and that, therefore, I would stop working (apparently forever), and that, therefore, it would not be in their best interest to hire me. They were looking for lawyers who would stay with the firm forever, justifying the faith and money reposed in them by the firm, which basically had to reeducate all new lawyers during their first two or three years on board.

The two firms which made me offers practiced a different form of discrimination. Both wanted me to specialize in areas which apparently had been found acceptable for women—one in real estate, and the other, either real estate or probate. The latter offer was made by the firm for which I had clerked the previous summer. My response was simply that I had no desire to specialize at that time. I had difficulty knowing which of the many areas of law I liked best, and I wanted an opportunity to explore as many as did the young men who joined the firm, recognizing that I would, eventually, wind up being a specialist if all went well. Fortunately, my inclinations proved acceptable, although not without the comment being made that the firm hoped my speciality would eventually turn out to be real estate or probate.

Nor was this the end of the discrimination. The starting salary rate at the top seven or so firms in Boston that year was $6,600. My starting salary was $5,600, which was clearly explained to me as being justifiable because no new lawyer really earned the full salary for the first two years while still being trained. During that time, the young lawyers were, in effect, subsidized by the firm. At the end of those two years, I was told, I would have married and would be home raising a family—therefore, I deserved no subsidy. No one told me whom I was going to marry, or what sex my children would be, but the outcome seemed clear to the firm otherwise.

Why was this acceptable to me? I really don't know. In later years I have sometimes been embarrassed that I was not one of the first to fight the system in the courts or in the legislature, but it simply never occurred to me. My only response at the time was to ask if I would be given a retroactive pay increase when I was still at the firm on my sixty-fifth birthday, a faithful (obviously single) associate. I never did get that promise. This initial salary discrimination continued for some years and grew, at least in one case I recall, to a discount of $1,500 for femaleness. I don't know whether a discount factor was applied to subsequent salary increases as the years went by because salaries were never discussed among associates, to the best of my knowledge.

In any event, I accepted the $5,600 offer and embarked on what I believed was going to be a general corporate practice. Two or three male lawyers started with the firm at about the same time. Precedent there indicated that all of us serve an apprenticeship in the blue sky (state securities law) field before moving on to federal securities practice. As the months went by and my apprenticeship dragged on, I suddenly realized that the firm had found another "acceptable" specialty for a woman lawyer. They had more than enough of this work to make me happy but, luckily, not enough to make it full time.

One of the very few rewarding aspects of blue sky practice was attendance at an annual convention, usually held in an attractive resort, where one could meet the various state securities commissioners, federal securities bureaucrats, and fellow sufferers in the blue sky field. It was at one of these conventions in Banff, Alberta, in 1967 that I met a significant number of employees of the Securities and Exchange Commission in Washington, D.C., and decided I had found my deliverance.

Despite my dislike for state securities work, I had seen enough of federal securities practice to believe that I would enjoy it enormously. For this reason I decided that a two-year stint at the SEC would give me the ammunition I needed to convince the firm to let a woman into this male stronghold. I had every intention of returning to the firm at the end of two years; indeed I was advised by a partner that anything more than two years would be counterproductive since I would probably acquire too many regulatory tendencies. Nowhere in all of this, by the way, was there any thought of partnership, no matter how successful my practice proved. There was only my desire for a more satisfying practice.

My acquaintanceship with several of the division directors at the SEC made my entry a little easier than for some. But despite seven years of private practice, I was offered only a GS-13 because in those days the Commission did not hire directly for a managing position, and a 13 was the highest grade for a non-management position. My first day on the job in Division of Corporate Regulation in April 1968 proved somewhat traumatic. I looked around and saw several women, but suddenly realized that they were no higher in grade than I. There was not then a single woman higher than a GS-13! Had I gone from the frying pan into the fire, with a reduction in salary to boot?

My own timing was apparently right. Within six months I was made the acting special counsel to one of the processing branches in the division, a position which was normally a GS-14, and which involved supervising several junior lawyers who reviewed registration statements, annual reports, proxy statements, and investment advisory contracts filed by or in connection with mutual funds assigned to each branch in the division. In addition to this disclosure work, the lawyers in the division reviewed the many applications filed by the funds and their investment advisers for exemptions or facilitating orders needed to comply with the rather arcane Investment Company Act and Investment Advisers Act of 1940. It was an opportunity to deal with some of the finest law firms in the country, which I found extremely satisfying, because with the power of the position I held came deference. Some of the people who, not so many years before, had refused me a position in their firm now recognized that it was within my power to grant or deny expeditious treatment of their application or filing.

In retrospect, I am glad that I had first had an opportunity to mature and see the other side of the process before being put in that position. Decisions involving millions of dollars were made daily at the branch level and delay of even a few days could be enormously costly. As the years went by, I supervised some lawyers, fortunately few in number, who, just graduated from law school, found the power thrust upon them—by supervisors too busy and over-burdened to spend the time training juniors—too much to handle wisely. They used their position to force compliance with unreasonable requests for changes in return for avoiding delay in effectiveness of a prospectus or other filing.

True to their promise, my supervisors made me a GS-14 special counsel when my first year was completed. This made me co-equal with the branch chief in the running of our branch, which included accountants and financial analysts as well as lawyers; it provided me with my first taste of administrative responsibility for the internal operation of the branch, as well as increased responsibility for the substantive work of the division. I believe at that time I was the only

GS-14 female in the entire Commission, although there may have been one other. The total labor force of the Commission was about 2,000.

After about a year and a half with the Commission, I was offered a position with a New York law firm by a junior partner who practiced regularly before the Division of Corporate Regulation. I wanted to explore this possibility, at least tentatively, since my self-allotted time for government service would expire within months. The firm seemed to be everything I had ever thought desirable. There was no talk of women doing anything different or less than the men, and while clearly a partnership was not in sight, I had the feeling that if I contributed as much as the men, I would be treated the same after an appropriate amount of time had elapsed. I later decided, however, that I had much more to learn at the Commission before I would be ready to call myself an expert, which is what I believed that firm wanted. So, I postponed my reentry.

Just about six months later, a legal assistant to one of the five commissioners asked me to fill in for a week while he was on vacation. To a young lawyer, these assistants had the best of all possible worlds. Each commissioner had responsibility for the work of the whole commission, and therefore, the sole assistant of each commissioner had an opportunity to learn and become involved in the work of the enforcement division, corporation finance division, public utility regulation division, opinions and review office, office of the chief accountant and so forth—in short, a great graduate course in securities regulation. The week actually turned out to be a test period to find a replacement for the soon-to-depart legal assistant. But all of my peers in the division advised against taking the position: It was seen as being beneath my level of expertise since most assistants were only two or three years out of law school when hired, and the maximum grade for an assistant was what I had already achieved, a GS-14. However, I decided that appearances of a lateral move, or in the opinion of some of my colleagues, a demotion, were not as important as the opportunity to learn more of the workings of the Commission and the practice of securities law—keeping in the forefront of my mind that I would soon be returning to private practice where a woman needed all the expertise she could garner.

I commenced this third phase of my career in July, 1970. The move proved very beneficial. Not only was I working for a commissioner who had none of the biases I had encountered in Boston, but I was in daily contact with the other commissioners (need I mention, all male at that time), their legal assistants (also all male), and the directors of all of the divisions. The work was very satisfying because, for the most part, only matters of major significance came to the Commission for decision. I was dealing with the most interesting questions of the day in securities law and had a hand in trying to formulate an appropriate solution. These were the days when the management problems of so many of the firms on Wall Street were threatening the integrity of the stock exchange system and destroying investor confidence. The commissioner for whom I worked played a major role in forging a solution which has lasted to this day. In all candor, however, one of the biggest pluses to this job as I now see it, was that I was exposed to the scrutiny of all of the major players at the Commission, which worked to my advantage when the time came for me to move on. That time came about six months later than I had wanted, because when I indicated a desire for a change, the commissioner said that he would be leaving in about six months; I deferred to his request to stay until he left in July 1972.

Four years with the government and facing an inevitable job change, I again thought the time would be right for private practice. Indeed, I was approached by several law firms who knew my job would be ending, and I engaged in exploratory talks with a couple of them. But again, for no easily articulated reason, I was not certain that I was ready to return. I had embarked on a government career with a very limited time horizon, yet I was having a wonderful time! For better or worse, the federal government is a critical player in most of the major events or our times, and in a senior government position, one feels at the very center of national policymaking.

While I was working for the commissioner, the grade level of a legal assistant had been raised to a GS-15, the equivalent at the Commission of an assistant director or chief counsel of a division. Clearly, I did not want to take a demotion, but it was hard to see where another GS-15 position was possible for me. But the chairman approached me with the news that the director of my old division was retiring. He proposed that I become the associate director, under a new director. The division was being reorganized, the disclosure function (that is, the work involving review of registration statements, updated prospectuses, annual reports, and so forth) was being transferred to the Division of Corporation Finance, and only the basic regulatory function remained with the Division of Corporate Regulation. Further, the division was being renamed the Division of Investment Management Regulation. Despite these changes, I was ecstatic; I was going home, this time as the number two person in the division.

The hours were long, with weekends almost invariably spent at the office, but I believed the experience would be invaluable. The director had no apparent difficulty with a female associate director, and other than some harmless teasing, I don't really believe it was ever a problem. A far more likely problem was his being given an associate director whom he had not chosen, but if this was ever so, he never let it show, either.

By this time, women at the Commission were on the move in just about every area. There was at least one other female legal assistant when I moved back to the division, and there were women branch chiefs, special counsels, and, I believe, even one assistant director of a division. When I received my GS-15 rating, I was only the second female ever to hold such a level in the history of the Commission, and my predecessor had since resigned. There still was discrimination at some lower levels, and many occasional practitioners before the Commission, not familiar with all the players, still often mistook any woman for a secretary or receptionist, but on balance, it was a good time to be female and be employed by the Securities and Exchange Commission.

I had found, after about 18 months as a legal assistant to a commissioner, that it is very difficult for me to live in the shadow of another person. Most times we had agreed on major decisions, but, of course, when we did not, his view prevailed—he had the vote. Naturally, the same was true of the relationship and power balance between a director and an associate director. Largely for this reason, after about two years on the job, I decided I needed another change. At just about the right time for me, the Commission established a National Market Advisory Committee, composed of experienced and respected members of the Wall Street community, whose function was to examine the structure and practices of the market and make recommendations for establishing a truly national market. The Committee was looking for a full-time executive director to take charge of its day-to-day work. It struck me that this experience would provide much more exposure to the trading and markets aspects of the Commission's responsibility than I had previously had, and would make me that much more valuable when I decided to return to private practice. Further, the life of the Committee was finite and if, as I suspected, I was having more than a little difficulty following my own advice about returning, the natural termination date of the job would force my hand. I was interviewed by the chairman of the Committee and eventually met with most of his senior associates.

When the position was offered to me, I went to the chairman of the SEC as a matter of courtesy to tell him I would like to accept. I was a bit dismayed when he kept telling me that I really didn't want it, but after a couple of weeks it became clear why he was saying this. He had decided to move my boss, the director of my division, upstairs to be a special assistant to the chairman, and I was to be his successor. Initially, I really did not want the position. I had spent enough time thinking about being executive director of the NMAC and talking with its members to be convinced that it would be a challenging and totally different job. I believed I was ready for that kind of dramatic change. However, I also believed then, and still believe now, that management responsibility for a large organization is the one area separating many female lawyers in government from their male counterparts and standing in the way of their advancement to higher policymaking echelons. With that thought in mind, yet still uncertain that the job was one I wanted, I decided to negotiate with the chairman about the conditions of the job—generally a very risky thing to do. However, it worked. I had told him that I believed the disclosure function was a critical part of the effective regulation of the industry and asked that the employees who had been transferred several years before to the Division of Corporation Finance to perform that function be returned to the Division of Investment Management Regulation. Further, I requested that responsibility for the new study of bank investment departments, just getting started, be lodged in my division as well.

I knew I could largely run my own shop. The division employed about 120 lawyers, accountants, financial analysts, and clerical staff. But because its responsibilities were being enlarged, the division was also allotted two associate directors, and after serious negotiations, I was given a free hand to select both of them. This was paramount to me. Under these circumstances I accepted the position, largely because of the management responsibilities, which proved to be stepping stones to my next position, as well.

I suppose that along the way during the next two years, there were men under me who resented working for a woman, and unfortunately, I know that several female secretaries wanted no part of a female supervisor. But these were basically inconsequential concerns to me. I might have bothered them, but they certainly didn't bother me. From the quarters that mattered in my estimation, I received as much respect and consideration as would any man in my stead.

But that doesn't mean it was a bed of roses, either. Running a division or an office that size anywhere, is not all fun and games. Management responsibilities do take time; hours that I often would have preferred to spend on substantive matters had to be devoted to administrative detail. I also have a suspicion that employees turn to a female supervisor with more problems than they would a male, expecting, I assume, a more sympathetic listener. Yet I believe that as long as this does not get too far out of hand, it can make a woman a more effective supervisor.

A phone call from a friend set the stage for my next move, one that proved my hunch about management responsibility. The general counsel of the Federal Home Loan Bank Board (the agency which regulates federally chartered savings and loan associations) had decided to move to the private sector, and the Board was seeking a replacement. A partner in my friend's firm did a lot of work in this field and knew that the chairman of the Board would like, everything else being equal, to have a female general counsel. Several women had been interviewed who were considered very bright, able attorneys, but none had been given the responsibility I had in running an office. The Office of General Counsel at the Board had some 55 lawyers and 30 secretaries. As a result, the very day I heard about the opening, the chairman made an offer to a male lawyer from, I believe, the private sector.

Because the offer was not immediately accepted, my friend

thought if I were interested, he would submit my name. I had not consciously thought about leaving the Commission for quite awhile, and I suppose if I had, I would have considered only private practice and not another government agency, especially one so seemingly removed from the practice of securities law. However, as soon as the question was put to me, I realized that I was bored. I had been director for just under two years, but had been in the mutual fund-investment adviser area for eight of my 10 years with the Commission. I agreed to have my friend submit my name, on the theory that at least it would make me go on an interview and consider alternatives to my present position. To make a long story short, the gentleman who had been offered the position turned it down, and I became general counsel of the Bank Board about two and a half months later. I think it is interesting here to note that although the chairman was a Democrat and a Carter appointee and I am a Republican, the position, traditionally somewhat political, was mine, largely because I am female.

What a challenge this opportunity turned out to be, and what an absolutely wonderful job is that of general counsel to a government agency, at least one with authority to litigate its own cases. Truly a lawyer's delight! And no, I was not completely away from a securities practice, for at that time the Board was seriously considering whether to allow savings and loan associations to become stock associations instead of operating in the traditional mutual form. This involved one of the most controversial opinions I was asked to render. In addition to a securities office, the general counsel was also responsible for a regulation office, an enforcement office, a litigation staff, a legislative staff, and a general division which rendered opinions on the many diverse questions concerning our controlling statute and its applicability in a time when savings and loan associations were scrambling to keep up with many new competing financial alternatives. All of the lawyers who worked for the Board were in the office of the general counsel, unlike the SEC, where each division had its own lawyers in addition to those in the general counsel's office.

Another major difference between the FHLBB and the SEC was the manner in which they were financed, and the resulting differences this made in operation. The SEC is financed out of the general treasury, whereas the FHLBB is financed out of assessments made against member associations. This makes money somewhat more available to the Board than to the Commission, and just before I arrived on the scene, the Board had been able to finance and build its own headquarters in downtown Washington, D.C. It had also managed to get authority to lease unused space in the building to commercial enterprises. I mention this because it added another wholly different dimension to my legal practice. The Office of General Counsel was responsible for leasing the space and for all the myriad other legal ramifications of a commercial landlord. It was something I had not bargained for, but again, it was part of making the position of general counsel of the Board, in my opinion, one of the best positions in Washington.

At the Board, just as at the SEC, women were on the move. The head of another office at the Board was female, and at least one of the assistant general counsel slots in my office was held by a female. By the time I had left both the Commission and the Board, each had its first female *member* to boot. Interestingly, and unfortunately, my relations with all of the office heads at the Board were cordial except those with the other woman director. I have never successfully analyzed why this was so, and it may have been merely a function of personalities having nothing to do with sex, but in my judgment it was particularly unfortunate precisely because we were both women.

Apart from this, however, I never had any reason to believe that my being female made any difference whatsoever in the way I was treated professionally. Oh, maybe there was a bit more gallantry on the part of the presidents of the various federal home loan banks throughout the country when they came to Washington, but this had no negative side effects. One very positive sidelight to this phase of my career was that I met my husband at the Board, where he was, for a short period following my arrival, the head of another office—clearly a positive aspect of being a woman in a professional role anywhere, not just in government!

Why then, if everything was so great, did I stay at the Board for only fifteen months? No, I was not yet bored (and don't think I would have been for some years to come) and no, I did not finally decide to return to the private sector. Again, I received a phone call from a friend, a law school classmate whom I had not seen for quite a few years. He was chairman of the Federal Communications Commission and knew that there would soon be an opening on the Commission for a Republican member. The departing commissioner was female, and the chairman was anxious to replace her with another woman. Was I interested, the chairman asked, in being put up as a candidate for presidential nomination to the seat?

In retrospect, I am almost embarrassed at how uncertain I was of my interest. As little as I knew about savings and loans, I knew even less about communications in general, and next to nothing about the jurisdiction of the FCC. I did know that I loved being a lawyer, and I was uncertain about how much law one really practiced at the commission level. Last, but most importantly, I had become aware how much power is exercised by high-level senior staff in any government agency. Much of the day-to-day authority of an agency is delegated to its staff, and only selected questions reach the commission level. As one of these seven at the FCC, I would get to make only one-seventh of each decision, and only on those matters brought to the Commission by its staff. I loved the staff power in even my limited area at the Bank Board. On the other hand, I was extremely flattered to be approached by the FCC at all—I think it was a phone call that comes to very few who have spent as many years as I have as a staff member with the government. Ultimately, I guess it was the challenge of a totally new arena and the prestige of possibly being appointed by the President of the United States to an important regulatory agency that tipped the scale.

Some months later, my name was submitted by President Carter to the Senate for confirmation as the fourth female member of the FCC, and confirmation came in March of 1979.

The work of the FCC has got to be the most intellectually stimulating and exciting of any agency in Washington. Technological innovation is pushing the Commission to find new and better ways to carry out its mandate to protect the public interest and to regulate "interstate and foreign commerce in communication by wire and radio so as to make available, so far as possible, to all the people of the United States a rapid, efficient, nation-wide, and world-wide wire and radio communication service with adequate facilities at reasonable charges . . . ." This must be done without the stifling delay and burden of unnecessary regulation that too often keeps the benefits of new technology from the public for years.

My term on the Commission will expire on June 30, 1985. Is it finally possible that after what then will be 17 years of government service, I will return to private practice? If I've learned anything about myself, it is that I am the worst procrastinator of my chosen destiny.

As for my long experience in government service, I would say that any discriminant treatment because of sex only worked in my favor. I like to believe that I was as qualified for any of the positions I held as any man would have been, but it is clear to me that I was noticed because I am female.

The only negative aspects of being female were things I heard about later. For example, when I first joined the Federal Communications Commission, I was asked (unfortunately by a young professional *woman*) if it was true that I had had an affair with the chairman of the SEC and, presumably, attained the level of director as a result. I have also been told that there was speculation that the chairman of the FCC and I had been more than simply good friends either while at law school or later, or both. These comments hurt, not so much because of their nature per se but more because they point to the fact that there still are many who do not believe women advance on their own merit.

I believe that women are moving up in government and, I perceive, in the private sector as well. But if anything was needed to convince me fully that we still have a long way to go, that proof arrived at my office just recently. I had been one of the principal speakers at a legal seminar sponsored by a non-governmental entity; the other speakers were lawyers and other professionals associated with the communications industry. As a gesture of appreciation for my participation, I received a thank-you note addressed to the Honorable Anne P. Jones. It began "Dear Mr. Jones," and was accompanied by a man's necktie.

CHAPTER 11

AS POLITICIAN:
Getting Into the Swing of Things

BY YVONNE B. BURKE

Nathansons Photography, Inc.

YVONNE B. BURKE

YVONNE B. BURKE

Fine, Perzik & Friedman
Los Angeles, Calif.

Education

J.D., University of Southern California School of Law, Los Angeles, 1956
B.A., University of California at Los Angeles, 1953 (political science)

Experience

Of Counsel, Fine, Perzik & Friedman, Los Angeles, July 1982-present
Partner, Kutak Rock & Huie, Los Angeles, 1981-June 1982
Member, Los Angeles County Board of Supervisors, 1979-1981
Partner, Kaplin, Livingston, Goodwin, Berkowitz & Selvin, Los Angeles, 1979
Congresswoman, U.S. House of Representatives, Washington, D.C. 1972-1979
State Legislator, California State Legislature, 1966-1972
Private Practitioner, Los Angeles, 1958-1966
Deputy Corporation Commissioner, California Corporation Commissioner's Office, Los Angeles, 1957-1958

Professional Activities

Admitted to practice in California, 1956
Member, UNESCO Commission, 1979-1982
Regent, University of California at Los Angeles, 1981-present
Member, Board of Trustees, University of Southern California, 1976-1981
Vice-Chairperson, Democratic National Convention, Miami, Fla., 1972
Member, Drafting Subcommittee of the Democratic Platform Committee, and *Chairperson,* Task Force on Foreign Defense Policy, Democratic National Convention, Chicago, Ill., 1976
Chairperson, National Democratic Committee on Platform Accountability, 1980-present

Publications

"Validity on Attempts to Rescind Ratification of the Equal Rights Amendment," *University of West Los Angeles Law Review,* Volume 8, summer 1976

Personal

Born: October 5, 1932, Los Angeles, Calif.
Married: 1957, for the second time, 1972
Children: One, born in 1973, and one stepchild

Chapter 11

AS POLITICIAN: GETTING INTO THE SWING OF THINGS

BY YVONNE B. BURKE

Many people make the decision to become a lawyer while they are in college, or afterwards when they become acquainted with the law. I made up my mind as a teenager. I decided to go into law because as I was growing up, civil rights cases were just coming to the public forefront.

I was particularly influenced by one case involving restrictive land covenants. The attorney who represented the plaintiffs won in the U.S. Supreme Court. I was also impressed by an attorney in a subsequent civil rights case, the famous Loren Miller. He was the uncle of a friend of mine. I followed his case in the newspapers with interest and appreciation. Later, when my friend had a birthday party at his uncle's home, I remember being on the patio and looking up at the second floor window where Miller was working. I saw all of the law books and I thought, "Oh, he must be working on something that is very important and will affect all of us." That's when I decided that I wanted to be an attorney too.

The only lawyer in my own family was a distant uncle, and I had very little knowledge of what an attorney really did except for what I read in the papers and saw on television. I probably visualized myself working at home as my mother did (she was a real estate broker), with an office on one side of my house. A metal plaque on the front door would say "Attorney at Law," but my life as a woman would never be interrupted. I would still be a mother and a wife; law would just be one other thing that I did. This was a very idealistic view of what my life as a woman attorney would be like, and of course it became very different as I grew older.

I received a great deal of encouragement from my family, even though at the time I was growing up there was only one black woman lawyer in Los Angeles, Martha Malone, and probably not over two in the whole state of California. When I was in college I got to know Martha because she was a member of the graduate chapter of my sorority and I went to her home for sorority events. Martha was very encouraging, even though she probably didn't believe me when I told her I wanted to become a lawyer, and she told me about her background and how she became a lawyer.

When I was in college, I had one thing in mind—to rush through so I could get into law school and get about my way as an attorney. I found that counselors at the University of California were not very encouraging to women, particularly black women, about going into law. Those counselors had never known a black woman lawyer, they certainly knew that none were in law firms, and they had no idea who would go to one with a legal problem. In fact, my counselor didn't know what kind of job to suggest for me, a political science major with a public administration specialty. I told him not to worry because I was going into law school.

I did go, and I found my experiences there very challenging. Very few women were in law school in the fifties. Only five were in my class. I remember particularly "Ladies Day," a day when only women would have to recite in class. That meant that during each class, for the entire hour, none of the men needed to worry about reciting their cases or reporting to the teacher on the subject being discussed. We women were called on, ostensibly, to make us tough so that when we would go into the courtrooms, we would not get upset. I have to look back on that experience and say it worked: I found that going out into the world as a litigator was not so stressful after all.

It is very difficult to explain to a woman coming out of law school today the opportunities—or rather the lack of them—for women lawyers in the late 1950's and the 1960's. When I was graduating from law school, women weren't even interviewed by the major law firms because very few of them were ever hired. A few of us were just beginning to go into large government offices, such as District Attorneys' offices and Attorney General offices. I joined the California Corporation Commissioner's offices as one of the first women deputy corporation commissioners.

But after a year, I found that I didn't really want to stay in government: I felt there were too many limitations on opportunities for doing some of the things that I wanted. So I went into private practice by myself. I was fortunate that I was able to purchase an active probate practice from a retiring lawyer and was thus able to survive financially. I also found work in a wide variety of other areas such as real estate, corporate, and family law.

The judges during those years had differing reactions to the women who came into their courtrooms. Some were very enthusiastic, greeted women warmly, and accepted the idea that most women would do a good job. However, others did not like the idea of women lawyers in the courtroom and were very skeptical of each one. These judges took it upon themselves to harass us whenever they could.

I practiced about 10 years before deciding to go into political life, and frankly, it was with the idea that I was going to continue my practice at the same time. I had no intention of ever giving that up. My decision to run for office was sparked by a few friends with whom I worked on the staff of the McCone Commission investigating the Watts Riots. Part of our job involved studying minority representation in the state and local governments, and then determining whether a lack of representation was related to the feelings of hopelessness and frustration that ultimately led to the riots. We found, in many instances, districts readily available for black representation where a minority member could easily have been elected. Ironically, at the time I concluded my work with the commission, a member of the State Assembly from my district became ill and was unable to run. So my friends from the commission convinced me to run. Within six weeks, I had declared my candidacy and was busy campaigning.

At that time, serving on the state legislature in California was a part-time job; however, a ballot proposition was also pending to make it full time. After I won the primary election, and was looking forward to going to Sacramento, both to become a state legislator and to continue practicing law, the ballot proposition passed. It thus became extremely difficult to move forward with a political career and continue my practice, but I went ahead into state government and still called myself a lawyer-legislator. I believe being a lawyer made a difference in my ability to run for political office—1966 was before the "Woman's Movement," and the ballot designation "attorney at law" somehow gave me an aura of confidence. It wasn't as important whether the candidate was a woman or a man—if he or she was an attorney the public assumed the credentials were there for the job. This helped me because when I went to Sacramento in 1967, there had never been a woman in the California State Senate, and there were only three serving in the legislature. Usually a great deal of skepticism followed women into the political arena.

In addition to helping me with my election, I found that once in politics, another asset of being a lawyer was an awareness of some of the important legal questions surrounding problems and concerns of the community, and a recognition of the inequities in our legal system. My approach in running for political office had, after all, been to campaign on some of those inequities: For instance, as a lawyer, I represented many people who had creditor problems, so I ran on a platform of eliminating prejudgement garnishments of wages (which ultimately came about through changes in the law). Through my law practice, I knew about the concerns and aggravations the public experienced, in particular those people who were poor and who often had problems meeting their obligations. So when I went to the capital, I already had the exposure and the legal training necessary to become an effective legislator. However, even though legislators deal with some of the same issues as lawyers, there's no question that it was certainly different than being a litigator or being involved in a corporate or real estate law practice.

Because I was a lawyer, I was assigned to the Finance and Insurance Committee, and there had probably my first awakening to the hardships of women in the legislature. Before I became a member, the committee members had often met at a private club during lunchtime to discuss the issues they were going to face in that afternoon's meeting. When I became part of the committee, however, a problem arose: The club did not allow women in at lunchtime because it was without a woman's powder-room attendant. Consequently, it was necessary for the committee to move its luncheon meetings to another place so I could take part in them. Ultimately we cancelled the luncheons. Another problem arose with the committee's dinner meetings because the club where those were held had a rule that women could only enter at night with a gentleman. So usually the chairman of the committee had to meet me and escort me into the club for those meetings.

Some people might say that women can't function in a legislative setting and become part of the inside workings of politics because they are not one of the gang, not one of the boys. I found, to the contrary, that it did not make a difference. If it is necessary to discuss a legislative problem, a woman can find a place to meet with people and do her job. The fact that a woman may be prevented from hanging out at the bars or gym with the guys doesn't prohibit her from being successful. However, it does seem to me that today, in the 1980's, women professionals should have the same access as men to those clubs and facilities.

Others might also wonder whether, as a woman, I had difficulty establishing rapport with voters. There is no question that some people in this country just say "I will not vote for a woman"; but in California I found enthusiasm and acceptance, particularly from women, while running for office. I used some of the same methods for raising money for my campaign as I had used for civil rights organizations and charities; I brought in the same friends with whom I had worked during charity fund-raising events. We raised the money in traditional ways such as small cocktail parties, barbecues—all the things you do when you're a mother raising money for the PTA—and it worked.

My bridge club was a good example of how women got into the swing of my campaign. The club bought a billboard, and the members were so pleased with having paid for it themselves, that every time they passed it they would say, "That's our billboard. We paid for that billboard to help Yvonne get elected to the legislature."

I have had some interesting experiences over the years analyzing my support from male and female voters. Generally, even when running for office in recent years, I have had a much higher level of support among women than among men. However, this differed in my last election after I had left Congress—a 1980 campaign for election to the Board of Supervisors of Los Angeles: In the largely white, conservative, blue-collar communities, I had more support from men than from women. I believe this reflected the belief of some housewives that women in the work force are competing with their husbands for jobs. Perhaps they have such a distorted picture of the women's movement, that they cannot relate to the career or professional women. For the most part, the strength for the women's movement has come from career, or upper class women, and many housewives, particularly lower income housewives, have not understood the need for women to achieve and move upward in professional areas.

Someone who has never been involved in politics must often wonder about the differences between the ways female and male politicians operate. Some say that women have not had the experience of team sports and, as a result, do not know how to work in the close team effort necessary for political circles. Of course, this depends on the woman just as much as it does on the man. There are some male politicians, just as there are female politicians, who never achieve the kind of team work and group effort necessary to be a leader in political circles, and there are some women who are quite adept at this.

I do think that there are some women who, even without the experience of close team cooperation, develop those same traits and function politically as if experts. I have seen women who are able to put together political machines and work closely with male and female politicians to establish a network of close political alliances. However, I must say that, if there is one skill in the political world in which very few women succeed, it's the art of moving up in the inner circles of political leadership. While some women work very well as whips or in caucuses, for the most part the average woman politician does not form close alliances with a small group of other politicians. She tends to operate as an individual, often focusing on individual issues which may or may not be of interest to her male counterparts.

But the name of the game in politics is having friends in the right places. A legislator must have the necessary alliances to get good committee assignments. The time has not yet come in politics when men feel guilty if there are no women participating in the inside political power structure. I found that the necessary friendships are not always along party lines, nor along philosophical or regional lines. Politicians often become very closely allied and friendly with people who have a very different kind of philosophy or political affiliations, but who are also interested in a particular subject or simply have a similar concern about an issue.

Although I personally never felt as a woman politician that I had any less clout or had to take a back seat to any male politician, the higher echelons of political life are still dominated by men. In fact, at this point, we don't have any women governors, although we hope to very soon. There are also very few women in the U.S. Senate, and very few in the top appointed policy-setting government jobs. But I feel confident that as more women go into politics, they will ultimately move up to the very highest levels. Women do a good job—they spend a lot of time, work hard, and realize that they have to be very prepared. If they aren't, they are easily criticized by those who say "Well, we knew a woman couldn't do the job anyway."

The ultimate question always is "What impact does being in politics have on your family and on your marriage?" I believe that politics is hard on all marriages, both for women and men politicians. The only difference is that as women, we are more sensitive to marital pressures resulting from political responsibility. We tend to pay more attention to this concern and we go out of our way to give time to children and husbands. Our male counterparts, on the other hand, are not successful in balancing family and political aspirations.

I was married after I left the state legislature and just before I went to Congress. When I married my husband, I had been in the legislature for six years and had just won my primary Congressional election. About a year or so later, we had a child. As a member of Congress, I commuted back and forth between Washington, D.C. and Los Angeles, with a child, every other week. It was not easy, but it was something that I wanted to do: I wanted to have children before I got too old, yet I also had a blossoming career, one that I found exciting and challenging. Somehow I managed to spend a great deal of time with my baby, probably because I planned it right and had her at a good time in the session. She was born the day after Thanksgiving, which gave me until the session started on January 15th to adjust. At least my daughter was old enough to travel before we started our difficult routine. I did find that it was possible to be a good member of Congress even with a small child. During the early years, I probably didn't make as many of the social events as I might have, because by the time I finished my Congressional duties, I wanted to go home to make sure my child was well cared for. I lived closer to the Capitol than I had previously because I wanted to be able to get home in 30 minutes in case of emergency. So while it was possible to have a child while I was in public office, my lifestyle changed as a result.

I found that when my daughter became older and began school, it became more difficult for me to travel back and forth. I remember once asking a pediatrician whether it was hurting her ears to travel on airplanes so much. He looked at me—and I could tell he was very critical of the fact that I traveled with my daughter—and he said "What you really should do, lady, is find some older woman and let her take care of your child so she will be in one place, and you can go about your career." My reaction was simple. I got another pediatrician. However, later there did come a time when I had to decide whether my child could continue leaving school early every other weekend to travel back to California with me. It was then that I considered going back to California to run for another office, which I ultimately did. I decided it would be better for me to be in one state or in one local office than to stay in Congress where it was necessary for me to travel 3,000 miles between my district and Washington. Thus I do believe that women in political office sometimes make decisions influenced by their concerns about marriage and family life.

I have had some very exciting times in political life, and it always makes me feel good when a young woman comes up to me and says, "I've decided that I want to become an attorney," or "I want to go into politics," or even "I decided that, even though I am over 35, I should have a child because I know that you have done it." Often I've felt that being in politics with high visibility is a burden, but there are many, many advantages. I've shared some of the details of my life that perhaps I would have preferred to be not quite so public, but in sharing them, I've assisted other women who might not have had the courage to take on a new career or political life, or even the courage to have children and balance family and career at the same time.

When young women ask me whether being a lawyer was an important part of my political career, I have to say it was, particularly as

I look back on my career in Congress, where I served for six years and was a member of the House Appropriations Committee. Many of the excellent projects I had, such as serving on the Assassination Committee, studying the assassinations of President Kennedy and of Martin Luther King, were assignments that came to me partially because I had a legal background and training.

I would encourage women who are interested in politics and in national and international issues to look at a political career. Even if you're not willing to run for political office, look at the idea of serving on a political staff, or as a political consultant, or even as a lobbyist. In these ways, too, you can have an impact on the political process. The true reflection of my feelings about a career in politics, however, is when I wonder whether I want my daughter to be in politics. I can't say that I would urge her either way: Her decision would have to be a very personal one.

But I will make it clear that I'd love for her to be a lawyer because I feel that has given me the choice of whether I wanted to be in politics or in business. The legal profession has provided me with alternatives. So I advise all young women who are looking at politics to look at the law as a stepping stone—as a method for moving into politics. Being a lawyer, for example, is one of the best ways to move into a staff position with someone who is in a local, state, or federal legislative office. Today the most direct route to political office is working on the staff of a person already there. The staff people for members of Congress or legislatures get to know sources for campaign money and have an inside line to those sources. Also, staff can still inherit political offices just as those who were part of the political machines during the 1940's and the 1950's moved into the offices by inheritance.

After six years in Congress, I decided to come back and run for Attorney General of California. I had a very successful race, but not successful enough. I lost in the general election by a small margin. I then went back to practicing law in a large entertainment firm, and I found the adjustment not as difficult as many would believe. Another of the strengths of being a lawyer when you have a political career is that there are many opportunities for the lawyer who has had political or government experience. Many other people who are in politics and are either defeated or decide to leave have a very hard time trying find a place for themselves out of political life. This is not true of a lawyer. Political expertise for an attorney is very useful today with all the red tape and difficulty in dealing with government problems. So even though I was in an entertainment firm, I found myself in its corporate department, handling municipal and government finance and working on legislative issues. The experience I had in government became very, very useful in trying to solve some of the problems related to these areas. I had occasion in many instances, when working on legislation, to go back and meet with some of my Washington, D.C. colleagues about the problems my clients were experiencing as the government applied some of those very laws I had helped place on our books.

But then, the same thing happened to me that happens to many people who have been in politics. I was offered an appointment in local government as a member of the Board of Supervisors of Los Angeles County. This was a position representing about one million people. There had never been a black member of the Board of Supervisors, nor had there ever been a woman member, so it was a very attractive offer. I knew it was a district where re-election would be very difficult because it was very conservative, with very few minorities, and had never before been represented by a Democrat. But I decided to give it a try for one reason: I knew that if I accepted the appointment, I would then be able to say that I had experience serving not only on the state but also on the local political level. I did serve in that position, found it very exciting, and learned a great deal.

But I did not win re-election when my appointment was up, so again I joined a large law firm, this time one where I worked primarily on municipal finance and administrative law problems. I have continued to work on tax exempt bonds, municipal finance, and administrative law in a subsequent firm. As a person who has served in government for many years, I can bring an understanding and insight to many of my clients on how government works. Of course, I do not separate myself from government totally. I work in many political campaigns. I serve as a Regent for the University of California where I continue to take part in local government and to be a part of that process.

The future of the lawyer who works in politics and government today is perhaps not as bright as it has been because we now see a cutting back on regulation and red tape, and many of those lawyers who specialize in administrative law don't have quite the volume of work and subsequent expertise that they had in the past. But there is still a very important role for the lawyer who has experience in government and who knows how to get things done. These lawyers can become lobbyists, or appear before state, local, or federal administrative agencies, assisting clients with the problems they have before those agencies. I'm sure there will always be a place for the attorney who has the background and understanding of how government really works.

CHAPTER 12

AS FEDERAL JUDGE:
Seeking Personal Balance and Public Service

BY DOROTHY W. NELSON

Timothy Galfas

DOROTHY W. NELSON

DOROTHY W. NELSON

United States Court of Appeals
Ninth Circuit
Los Angeles, Calif.

Education

LL.M., University of Southern California Law Center, 1956

J.D., University of California School of Law (Los Angeles), 1953; Order of the Coif, Phi Kappa Phi

A.B., University of California (Los Angeles), 1950; Phi Beta Kappa (political science)

Experience

United States Circuit Judge, United States Court of Appeals for the Ninth Circuit, Los Angeles, 1980-present

Faculty Member, USC Law Center, 1957-1980 (joined as Instructor, 1957; appointed Assistant Professor, 1958; appointed Associate Professor, 1961; appointed full Professor, 1967; appointed interim Dean, 1967; appointed Dean, 1969)

Attorney, solo practice, Los Angeles, 1954-1980

Professional Activities

Admitted to practice in California, 1954

Member, American Bar Association (chairman, Committee on Education in Judicial Administration, 1972-1980; member, Sections on Judicial Administration and on Family Law; member, Committee on Resolutions, 1973; member, Long-range Planning Committee, 1979)

Fellow, American Bar Association

Member, American Law Institute

Member, American Judicature Society (member, Executive Committee, 1976-present; Board of Directors, 1972-1975, 1976-present; Research Advisory Committee, 1974-present; Editorial Advisory Board, *Judicature,* 1974-present; Vice-President, 1977-1979; Chairman of the Board, 1979-1981

Member, Association of American Law Schools (Member, Committee on

Education in Judicial Administration, 1973; Chairman, Committee on Education in Judicial Administration, 1976-1980; Member, Nominating Committee and Program Committee, 1972)

Member, Supreme Court Historical Society, 1976-present

National Vice-President, Order of the Coif, 1974-1976

Board of Directors, Constitutional Rights Foundation, 1971-present

Member, Committee of the Judicial Conference of the United States to Consider Standards for Admission to Practice in the Federal Courts, 1976-1979

Member, Nominating Committee, Los Angeles County Bar Association, 1979

Advisory Board, National Center for State Courts, 1971-1973

Member, Los Angeles County Bar Association (Committee on Economical Litigation, 1975-1980; Chairman, Subcommittee on Community Mediation, 1976-1979)

Member, World Association of Lawyers, World Peace Through Law Center

Member, Los Angeles Women Lawyers' Association

Appointed by President Carter to the White House Commission on Pensions Policy, 1979

Appointed by President Ford to the Board of Visitors, U.S. Air Force Academy, 1976

Appointed by President Nixon to the White House Conference on Children, 1970

Publications

"Carter's Merit Plan: A Good Step," 61 *Judicature* 105 September 1977

"Admission to the Federal Bar—The Work of the Devitt Committee," *Association of Business Trial Lawyers,* April 1977

Judicial Administration and the Administration of Justice, West, 1975

"The Role of the Trial Judge in Clinical Legal Education," 13 *The Judges' Journal* 20 (1974)

"Variation on a Theme—Selection and Tenure of Judges" (Symposium on Judicial Administration) 36 *Southern California Law Review* 4 (1962)

"Should Los Angeles County Adopt a Single Trial Court Plan?" 22 *Southern California Law Review* 117 (1960)

Holbrook, James G., *Survey of Metropolitan Courts—Los Angeles Area* (University of Southern California, 1956, Dorothy W. Nelson senior research associate)

Personal

Born: September 30, 1928, San Pedro, Calif.
Married: 1950
Children: Two, born in 1958 and 1961

Chapter 12

AS FEDERAL JUDGE: SEEKING PERSONAL BALANCE AND PUBLIC SERVICE

BY DOROTHY W. NELSON

Growing up in an active family with a sister two years older and one two years younger, with a career mother (teacher-psychologist) and a supportive father (building contractor), there was never a question whether my sisters and I would go to college and have a career—only which college and which career. My high school counselor did say to me: "Dear, what are you going to do *until* you get married?"—totally disregarding the possibility that by the time my youngest child would be in school full time, I might still have 30 to 40 productive years ahead. But my mother was my model, so the counselor's question did not change my goals. My mother, while placing family first at all times yet pursuing actively her own career interests, had demonstrated that with the proper balance, a woman could do both happily and productively.

When I was in the eleventh grade, I was a YMCA counselor (in 1945, there was still a post-war shortage of men), and I had a group of 18 underprivileged eight-year-old boys called the "Gorillas." My love for children led me to the tentative conclusion that I wanted to be a social worker helping young people. But I soon found that when I tried to help a family get more state aid, or have a child transferred out of a poor school environment, I was met with retorts of "the law won't permit it" or "a judge would never make a favorable ruling in this case." It appeared to me that lawyers and judges had a great deal of power in the community, far more than a social worker in terms of bringing about needed changes. So I decided to look toward law school.

Not long after that, a "Girls' Week" program in California strengthened my resolve. I participated by playing the role of a judge in the Juvenile Court of Los Angeles County. The woman judge who actually held that position, and several women lawyers, later invited me to their offices and encouraged me greatly to pursue law as a career.

Another, even more important event, occurred while I was counseling the "Gorillas." Another counselor, James F. Nelson ("Jim"), led the "Cherokees," a second group of eight-year-old boys. His love for children, his leadership qualities, his acceptance of me as a co-equal, and his commitment to the betterment of the community attracted me to him, in more than professional ways. Unfortunately, his notice of me was totally professional at that time (I did wear braces), but we were to meet again in a YMCA summer camp after our first year in college, and have been together since. He was at Stanford and I was at UCLA. He quickly transferred.

In the late forties, all college counselors advised students who were interested in law to major in political science, which I did. Reflecting back on that advice, my experience as a law student, lawyer, law professor, law dean, and judge has led me to conclude that an English major is preferred over all others—although any major is permissible if you work hard and force yourself to take courses which require extensive writing.

My acceptance at the UCLA Law School didn't surprise me: I thought that my grades and test scores were competitive for consideration in that class, only the second at the UCLA Law School. What was unexpected was that I was only one of two women in a class of approximately 90. Yet rather than feeling discriminated against, I always felt special and extremely well-treated and accepted by my classmates. One incident of particular importance, which helps explain why I felt this way, involved membership in a professional legal society. Members of my first-year law class were invited to sign up, but some weeks after joining, we received word from the group's national officers that all were welcome except the two women and one black in the class. (Note that this was in 1950, before *Brown v. Board of Education* .) The president of the class called us together and said that he felt "outraged" at this response; he thought all should resign and form the UCLA Legal Association. And that is what the class did.

When I approached our class president to thank him for unifying the class, I asked him why he had done this. He had been a friend in undergraduate school, but was never inclined to speak out, particularly on social issues. He replied that he was attending meetings of the Baha'i Faith, a world religion dedicated to the principle of the oneness of humanity, to the abolition of prejudice of all kinds, and to recognition of the equality of men and women. He asked if I'd like to attend a fireside meeting, and I quickly responded (as a good Episcopalian), "No thank you, but I'm glad it works for you."

Little did I know then what a profound effect that one conversation would have on my life. Two weeks later, my husband and I left a bridge game with the class president to attend a Baha'i Fireside. This in turn led to a five-year study of comparative religions, after which we both became members of the Baha'i Faith.

When I graduated from law school, Roscoe Pound, dean emeritus of the Harvard Law School and distinguished professor at UCLA, recommended me for a research position on a trial court survey of Los Angeles County, sponsored by the American Bar Association. I was to work with a law professor at the University of Southern California Law Center and other recent law graduates. We were offered a scholarship for an LL.M. degree plus $250 a month. My classmates who were starting with law firms at $350 a month thought I was lacking sound judgment to accept such low pay, but I liked the university atmosphere and the idea of receiving an advanced degree. I felt totally unqualified to practice, despite my degree, and in the research position I was permitted to have my first clients on the side as long as I worked a 40-hour week.

I have never regretted this decision, for without knowing it, I became one of the first experts in judicial administration in the United States—a field concerned with how justice is really administered, and what alternatives exist for improving the system. Dean Pound had often said to us in class that it really didn't matter so much what the laws were if the process by which the laws were enforced was ineffective; the system would not work. My new expertise led to an invitation to teach judicial administration at the USC

Law Center when the professor for that course was called away to Europe. My special knowledge enabled me to give a unique program, including field trips, ranging from the drunk arraignment courts to the California Supreme Court, and a class interview with Justice Tom Clark of the United States Supreme Court. The students urged the dean to hire me, and in 1957 I became a full-time instructor, the first full-time woman member of the USC law faculty.

Once again, I felt no discrimination, but rather an acceptance, even a favored status by the dean, faculty, and students. I must say that I did a great deal of entertaining during those days, especially after my son arrived in the summer of 1958, so the faculty wives could see that I was happily married (i.e., not after their husbands), and as anxious to befriend them as their husbands. I think this prevented certain tensions, queries, and speculation that might otherwise have occurred.

When my son was born, I felt the first real conflict in my life. I was then an assistant professor of law, teaching from late September to the end of May, approximately six hours a week. I wondered if I should continue on or drop out for five years until my son was in school most of the day. I naturally questioned whether I could find someone suitable to take my place while I was at work. But after interviewing over 90 applicants—who ranged from the "I teach them to mind" to the "You'll never see a spot on the rug" types—I found a loving new member for our family. We called her "Nana," and she worked for us over 13 years. Although there were occasional spots of dust here and there, she truly served as our extended family, and with her help I had the best of both worlds. I never taught during the summer, had five weeks off between semesters, and did most of my class preparation at home (sometimes burning the midnight oil). While "Nana" lived near, she did not live in, and Jim and I did all of our own cooking—whoever got home first started the dinner. I was able to participate in a part-time cooperative nursery school, and along with my children, had all the fun of ballet lessons, music lessons, Girl Scouts, and school projects. This gave balance to my life, which I think made me a better teacher.

Of course, the key ingredient to this satisfying combination of work and home life was my husband and our mutual commitment to our religious beliefs. As Baha'is, we believe that our purpose is to know and love God and to carry forward an ever-advancing civilization; to assist each other in service to mankind; and to maintain the family as the central and most important unit of society. These beliefs helped us keep our priorities straight and gave us a common sense of purpose.

My tenure on the faculty was particularly happy because I enjoyed interacting with students and student organizations, such as the Great Issues Forum, Student Bar Association, Law Review, and Moot Court Board. This predilection probably led to my selection as assistant dean, then associate dean (where I focused on faculty recruitment and curriculum development), and finally dean. I later learned that some of the alumni were unhappy about the choice of a woman dean, but I felt strongly supported by the faculty, students, university administration, and most alumni during my time in the job. My hope was to provide an atmosphere of support so each person could develop fully, whether faculty member or student. Thus my goal was to bring out of diversity school unity.

Once again, support from my family was crucial. I attended many night meetings for fund-raising events and accepted new appointments to national committees and posts—such as the White House Conference on Children, the President's Commission on Pensions, the Board of the Air Force Academy, the Board of the American Judicature Society, and the ABA Committee on Judicial Administration—to assist our school and promote its national reputation. Still other community responsibilities included serving on the boards of directors for the Federal Reserve Bank, Southern California Edison, and Farmers Insurance Co. With such a long list of commitments, all members of the family had to pitch in with meals and household chores, even though we still had "Nana"; but the family also enjoyed the benefits of this busy schedule, such as trips abroad to my various meetings. We also continued to participate together in the activities of the Baha'i Faith (Sunday school, summer camp, Jim and I serving on the National Assembly), which further strengthened our family life.

When I was approached in 1979 by President Carter's Merit Selection Commission on the Federal Judiciary and was asked if I wished to be considered for an appellate court judgeship, I wasn't sure how to respond. The USC Law Center had attained ranking among the top schools in the nation, my family was happy, my salary was excellent, and I enjoyed my work. On the other hand, I was tired of fund-raising, and as a supposed expert in judicial administration, I had always wondered what it would be like to be a judge. Since Jim was then a state court judge, I did know some of the inside information on the inner workings of the courts, but I thought it would be interesting to learn more. Moreover, I had been a long-time admirer of Judge Shirley Hufstedler, then the only woman on the United States Court of Appeals, (who later became the first United States Secretary of Education). My one fear was that the work of an appellate judge would isolate me from community affairs, in which I had a great deal of interest, but observing Shirley, I realized that this did not have to be so. She participated actively in local, national, and international affairs.

Also influencing my decision was a strong belief that until women attain high policymaking positions, the very peace of the world is at stake. When meeting with Mrs. Jehan Sadat in Cairo, Egypt, in 1975, prior to our participation in the U.N. Conference on Women held in Mexico City, we had agreed that not only was the education of women important, but that it was also necessary for world peace. She told the story of the Jewish mother who had written to her after the 1973 war between Egypt and Israel, which the Egyptians won. The woman wrote to Mrs. Sadat, not as the wife of President Sadat, but to her as a mother. The Jewish mother said that her only son had been captured in the war, her husband had been killed, and she had no one to care for her. She pleaded with Mrs. Sadat to find her son and send him home. Not only did Mrs. Sadat find the son and send him home, but she published (against the advice of her husband's ministers) an open letter in *The Jerusalem Post.* It said that from one mother to another, she was returning the son to his home, and that until we, the women of the world refuse to give up our sons and daughters to war, we will have no peace. When President Sadat later made his trip to Israel, and stepped out of the plane at David Ben-Gurion Airport, Mrs. Sadat was not physically present, but her influence was deeply felt. Experiences like this one made me realize that I, too, had to try to do my part in serving our greater goals.

My tenure on the court has been interesting, educational, and sometimes exciting. My circuit is the largest (23 active judges) and has more women (three) than any other. In 1981, when I participated on the first Court of Appeals all-woman panel (we sit in groups of three) in the history of the United States, presiding Judge Betty Fletcher, of the state of Washington, noted the significance of the event and expressed her hope that more women will be appointed to the bench in the future. There are now 12 women out of 155 appellate court judges in this country.

Just as when I was dean, I have felt well treated and respected by my judicial colleagues. And as far as I can determine, the litigants do not complain about the women judges on our court. Some of the judges have remarked that the women promote more collegial events than the men, such as luncheons and dinners, but others do not make any comments about our influence as women per se.

The women judges, just like the men, have diverse backgrounds, which undoubtedly affect their approach to cases. We react to litigants, lawyers, and other judges accordingly. The fact that we are women has affected our life experience and has naturally determined certain qualities and attributes which we bring to the bench. As a Baha'i, I look upon men and women as two wings of a bird. Unless they are both strong and compelled by a common force, the bird cannot fly heavenwards. But, if you will take note, you cannot tear off the right wing of a bird and insert it into the socket of the left wing. Both wings have certain common qualities, but also certain unique qualities which are special and different. In some cases, it may be the nurturing quality of a woman who has experienced motherhood, or in the case of a man, a different quality. Both are needed to provide the correct balance.

As I have been supported and encouraged throughout the years by both women and men, it is my hope that I may assist those who wish to succeed in the profession or any aspect of their lives. My current plans are to remain in this professional role for the rest of my life, but as in the past, I have found it wise not to make permanent plans. As long as I am able to apply my knowledge constructively and express my love for humanity, I shall be happy.

CHAPTER 13

AS LAW PROFESSOR:
The Practically Perfect Job

BY LILLIAN R. BEVIER

Marianne Sullivan

LILLIAN R. BEVIER

LILLIAN R. BEVIER

University Of Virginia
School of Law
Charlottesville, Va.

Education

J.D., Stanford Law School, 1965; Order of the Coif; Revising Editor, *Stanford Law Review;* Hilmer Oehlmann, Jr., award for excellence in the first year legal writing program

B.A., Smith College, 1961 (government)

Experience

Professor of Law, University of Virginia Law School, 1973-present

Associate Professor of Law, University of Santa Clara Law School, 1970-1973

Associate, Spaeth, Blase, Valentice & Klein, P.C., Palo Alto, Calif., 1968-1970

Research Associate, Professor William Baxter, Stanford University Law School, 1966-1968

Assistant to the General Secretary and Assistant Legal Counsel, Stanford University, 1965-1966

Professional Activities

Admitted to practice in California, 1966; *in Virginia,* 1979

Editorial and Program Consultant to Virginia Local Government Attorneys Association, 1980-present

Member, planning committee, Association of American Law Schools, and group discussion leader, Property Law Teachers Conference, Charlottesville, summer 1982)

Consultant, Joint Land Use Task Force of the Virginia Association of Counties and Virginia Municipal League, January 1980-May 1981

Assistant Dean for Students, University of Virginia Law School, January-June 1978

Lecturer on Land Use, University of Virginia, Continuing Education of the Bar Summer School for Lawyers, 1977

Faculty Member, Association of American Law Schools (AALS) Law Teaching Clinic, Sacramento, Calif., summer 1976

Chairman, State Bar Local Administrative Committee No. 2(a) for Santa Clara County, 1972-1973

Member, Stanford University Law School Board of Visitors (Committee on the Status of Women at the Law School, 1972-1974)

Hearing Officer, Stanford University Campus Judicial Panel January-March 1972

Member, Economic Opportunity Commission, Santa Clara County 1968-1969

Publications

"Justice Powell and the First Amendment's Societal Function: A Preliminary Analysis," 68 *Virginia Law Review* 177 (1982)

"Like Mackerel in the Moonlight: Some Reflections on *Richmond Newspapers,*" 10 *Hofstra Law Review* 311 (1982)

"An Informed Public, An Informing Press: The Search for a Constitutional Principle," 68 *California Law Review* 482 (1980)

"The First Amendment and Political Speech: An Inquiry into the Substance and Limits of Principle," 30 *Stanford Law Review* 299 (1978)

Book Review of Donahue, Kauper & Martin, *Property: An Introduction to the Concept and the Institution,* 73 *Michigan Law Review* 620 (1975)

"Legal Aspects of Airport Noise," 15 *Journal of Law & Economics* 1 (1972); (under the name of Lillian Altree; in collaboration with Professor William Baxter of Stanford University Law School)

Personal

Born: June 11, 1939, Washington, D.C.

Married: 1962; for the second time, 1975

Children: Three, born in 1963, 1966, and 1979

Chapter 13

AS LAW PROFESSOR: THE PRACTICALLY PERFECT JOB

BY LILLIAN R. BEVIER

Resumes are rather barren documents—people don't tend to spring to life from pages printed with facts. My own resume, for example, accurately describes my progress from college to law school to law teaching, and it lets you know that I am presently married for the second time and the mother of three children. But I can't help feeling that there are some important facts about me that you might overlook.

Notice that, I have now been teaching rather a long time—more than 10 years. If I had been asked to write this chapter five years ago, I might very well have said quite different things. But time has had a way of dimming my memory for unpleasant facts. More importantly, it has had a way of ironing things out: Difficulties and problems that bothered me intensely five years ago have now diminished in importance—not because I have learned to accept them as my fate but because I have learned better ways of dealing with them.

Also notice that, I went to college in the 1950's and law school in the early 1960's—before the women's movement began to take root in society's consciousness. The more I reflect on my professional experiences, and on my reactions to those experiences, the more certain I become that many of my own attitudes were irrevocably shaped—for good or ill— by the social norms that prevailed when I was growing up. Attitudes are different now, so my daughter will develop different expectations about herself and how she ought to fare in a professional setting. But I *expected* things to be exceptionally difficult for me as a woman lawyer. If pressed, I probably would have said that it wasn't fair that I should be so burdened, but I didn't think about it much. I was prepared to hoe a more difficult row so long as I wasn't kept out of the garden entirely. I had no reason to believe that any sense I had about being treated unfairly would eventually be widely shared by society. Attitudes toward women lawyers seemed firmly entrenched—and I wasn't a prophet.

I was one of only five women in my Stanford Law School class. There were no women professors at Stanford then, and precious few women lawyers out in the world to provide any sort of "role model" for us. With hindsight, the five of us seem like pioneers, since many women have followed in our wake. But at the time, we had no idea we were on the crest of a wave, and we certainly didn't think of ourselves as being part of—much less leaders of—an important social movement. Each of us had simply decided that a career in law was what she wanted, and each was willing to risk being thought a little weird in order to pursue her own goals.

Occasionally during law school classes my mind would wander from the subject being taught to the man teaching it. I would speculate about his job and what it would be like to have it. I knew that each of my professors had graduated near the top of his law school class. But, apart from the fact that they were expected to teach classes, I was profoundly ignorant of what they actually *did.* I liked law school and learning about the law, so I rather envied the professors their superior knowledge. I guessed that they liked their work a lot, though I often wondered how they handled being so exposed and vulnerable—students staring at them, judging them, trying to outsmart them day after day.

I didn't try to imagine myself doing what they did. While I assumed that I could do anything in law that I wanted to do, it had never occurred to me to become a professor.

But after I had been out of law school for five years and had practiced law for two (I'd had two other legal jobs before going into practice), I began to feel that it was time to change the direction of my career. I decided to look for a job more suited than practice to my particular talents and inclinations. Practice had been frustrating for me, primarily because it involved short-term problem solving without much opportunity to think about the systematic implications of the rules. "Justice" in the abstract doesn't matter much to a client who's paying the bills!

It just so happened that about the time I decided to start looking for something different, there was an opening for the coming academic year at the University of Santa Clara Law School. On the perceptive advice of one of my former Stanford professors, I applied, and I was hired. (The advice was perceptive because he discerned my latent professorial bent before I myself had any notion of it.) What luck! Santa Clara is a fine regional law school. Although not among the top ten law schools in the country, it attracts very bright students and, when I started teaching there, it had begun to build a strong young faculty. For three years I taught there and loved it. It would be impossible to imagine being treated with more kindness or generosity than I was by both the students and the faculty at Santa Clara. A young, first-time teacher can expect to make some horrible blunders in the classroom, and I certainly made my share, but the students at Santa Clara were almost unfailingly forgiving and supportive.

In retrospect, I am rather amazed that being a woman was not more of a handicap to my teaching at Santa Clara. Most of the students there were quite unused to women professors, and the influx of women students into law schools had not yet begun. The students were certainly not unaware or uninterested in my being female. My nickname, I later learned, was "Legs." Once, when I called upon a student to recite a case in class, he confessed that while he had nothing to say about the case, he did think that the sweater I was wearing was awfully attractive! When I left Santa Clara, the students in one of my classes bid me farewell with a beautiful necklace and earrings—hardly an appropriate gift for a man. Experiences like these might have been disquieting to someone whose consciousness had been raised to a more sensitive level than was mine. They do suggest that the students thought of me differently because I was a woman. But the students generally took me seriously; they were attentive and respectful in my classes. Consequently, I would have been hard put to find real cause for alarm just because they sometimes responded to me as a female!

After three years at Santa Clara, I decided it was time to move on.

I was making progress as a teacher, but I needed a more demanding environment. For example, I had been awarded tenure at Santa Clara, though I had not yet written—much less published—a word of scholarship. I felt I needed to be at a place where I would find stronger encouragement for my scholarly ambitions. So in 1973, when I was invited to become a visiting professor at the University of Virginia, I accepted almost without hesitation.

Looking back, I am quite frankly stunned at my nerve! Of course it is easy to see why I was tantalized by the fine reputation of the law school, but Charlottesville, Va., was 3,000 miles away from home and I knew no one there. My two boys, who were then 10 and 7, loved California and were not eager to leave. I knew they would miss their father—we were divorced but he and the boys were very close. My friends at Santa Clara teased me about responding to the lure of the big leagues, and a colleague here at Virginia later remarked that my move could only be explained as "the triumph of ambition over self-interest."

Life here at Virginia has not been without its moments of loneliness and frustration, and the intellectual challenge has on occasion seemed intimidating: My colleagues are very smart and so are the students. But I have never regretted the decision to try my wings here. There has been more warmth than loneliness, more satisfaction than frustration, and more fun than intimidation in the challenge.

After a year at Virginia as a visiting professor, I was offered a tenure-track position. In the fall of 1977, after I had written a scholarly article, I was awarded tenure—the first woman to receive it at the University of Virginia Law School. (Unfortunately, I still am the only woman on the permanent faculty. We have extended offers to a number of women, but each decided, for one reason or another, not to come to Charlottesville.) My memory has been kind enough to lapse about the details of those pre-tenure years between 1974 and 1977. One very happy event took place—my marriage in 1975—but professionally it was a hard time for me. Tenure-track is difficult any place, whether you're male or female: You feel as though you're under constant scrutiny (even though, of course, you're really not), and the pressure to perform seems unrelenting. Even when you're getting moderately positive signals from colleagues and students, you may be inclined to have your antennae wired to receive or exaggerate negative responses. About all I felt I could do during that period was to try to maintain my dignity as I lived through it, hope that it would turn out all right, and then put it behind me the *minute* it was over.

Tenure, once you have it, is wonderful. It is the ultimate in job security. Still, for me, 1977 seems to mark only the beginning of my career as a law professor. I continue to approach every aspect of my job as though I need to earn tenure anew. I suppose that's because I'm a compulsive type of person—though it might also be because I can hardly believe my good fortune.

I love my job. It doesn't pay as well as private practice, but it doesn't carry the same pressures either. I get to think about things that *I* think are interesting, rather than spending time worrying about whichever client's problem happens to be on the top of the pile on my desk. I also like having a working schedule almost entirely my own. As a married woman law professor with children, I have to meet—somehow or other—a number of often conflicting demands on my time, energy, and emotional commitment. Any married woman with children and a career confronts these conflicts. We all are too often plagued by the nagging doubt that, whatever it is we are doing at one minute, *we probably should be doing something else.* But I have built-in "flextime." This doesn't mean that I don't have to work lots of hours, but it does mean that I can work them when it suits my needs. I have been able to be home either all day or for large chunks of it when I was needed there most, and still get my other work done by working late into the evening. I've been very tired more than once, but nevertheless I have been able to schedule my work to fulfill both commitments.

The job of a law professor is, like Gaul, divided into three parts: teaching, scholarship, and a variety of other academic duties that are neither teaching nor scholarship. For want of a better word, I'll call this third area the "collegial" part of the job. This label at least suggests the nature of the tasks involved.

Each part of the job presents special challenges. As I reflect on my own experience in each, I think I can identify some ways in which my being female affected either how I was perceived by others or how I perceived myself. I don't suppose that all or even many women would interpret or react to my experiences the way I do, and I could not begin to speculate (without making a complete fool of myself) how my experiences would have been different "if I'd been a man." But I will try to describe the pressure points that seemed to me to come from being a woman, and perhaps that will help identify issues that might be of special concern to women law teachers generally.

Teaching

Most people are probably familar with the stereotypical law school professor: Professor Kingsfield of "Paper Chase" fame. And, as in many stereotypes, there is a little bit of truth in the Kingsfield characterization. Many law school classes are taught "Socratically" using the case method. That is, the students read an assigned number of appellate cases, the professor asks questions about the cases, and individual students are called upon to respond. At its best, this method is surprisingly effective as a device for conveying legal principles, for developing analytical skills, and for teaching young lawyers how to think on their feet. At its worst, it can degenerate into a tool by which a professor can intimidate or humiliate students. Even in the hands of a benign master of the technique, the method tends to generate a highly charged, competitive classroom atmosphere. Perhaps because law school classes mirror the legal system which they are designed to teach, they tend to have an adversarial tone, with teachers and students seemingly locked in uneasy mental combat, attempting to prove to one another their intellectual worth and the relative power of their ideas.

The intellectual task of teaching is no different for me than for my male colleagues. I, too, have to learn "the law" and attempt to present or package the day's material in a coherent and thought-provoking way. Male or female, we all confront the same technical problems in deciding what material to cover, what perspective to take, what questions to ask, what pace to set, and what order to pursue. I have male colleagues who seem as tense and uneasy before class as I do—who can't eat breakfast before a morning class, for example. Still, I think the challenge of the classroom for me has often been more formidable. I seem to spend more hours getting ready and to waste more energy worrying. If so, I'm like a lot of women law professors: A recent study indicated that, on an average, we prepare longer for class than our male colleagues.

I got a clue to why this might be so from an unusually perceptive colleague who once visited several of my classes. He was there to evaluate my performance as part of Virginia's tenure process. Later, we talked about what had gone on. He made a few comments about the substance of what I had done—wondering why I had pursued a certain line of inquiry, and questioning the wisdom of spending a long time on a point that he did not consider particularly important. I've actually forgotten most of what he said along these lines, because I was so struck by his observation about how strange the class *felt* to him. He'd never had a woman professor, and had never sat in on a woman's class before. "Y'know," he said, "it's really *different.* There's a sort of 'prove-it' atmosphere—as though they're waiting in ambush to catch you in a mistake. It must make things uncomfortable for you!"

It may seem odd, but my principal reaction to this comment was one of relief. "Ah," I thought. "So *that's* it!" I had sensed a sort of resistance to my classes, and had struggled to overcome it in a variety of ways. When I learned that I wasn't imagining it, I was reassured—at least I wasn't crazy! I still felt somewhat powerless to deal with the problem. I couldn't force a change in attitudes toward women that had been years in the making. However, I could—and did—stiffen my resolve to be an effective teacher, and I've noticed that the atmosphere in my classes now seems less resistant to these efforts. But I still prepare like mad.

During the time right before class I am at my least graceful. The other day, for example, I was in my office. It was ten minutes to eleven, and class was at eleven. There was a knock on my door. "Come in!" I barked. It was a member of the dean's staff who'd been sent round to poll the faculty on some issue or other. She asked me, innocently enough, "Have you got half-a-second?" I positively snapped at her in reply. "Well, I suppose I've got half-a-second. But no more. *I've got class in ten minutes!*" My only excuse for being so rude to her was that she had come upon me at such an unpropitious time. It didn't matter that I was long-since well-prepared, that I had taught the material twice before in previous years without particular difficulty, or that I am an experienced teacher with one or two tricks of the trade up my sleeve. I know that my reaction to this momentary interruption was quite irrational, but this is the way I *always* feel before *any* class. The feeling is a little like stage fright, just as law teaching is a little like acting. Only with law teaching, there's no script and no director—no prompter and no fellow actors. There's just you and the audience of students. I sometimes wonder how I have the courage to do it day after day—and if it weren't for the fact that I love it, I'd surely quit tomorrow.

I once saw myself described in print as a "beautiful but stern" law professor. To me, this description (never mind whether it is true) captures a sense of the thin line I've sometimes felt I was walking, especially when I first started teaching. On one side is the risk of being too attractive to be taken seriously, and on the other side is the danger of becoming too serious to be considered attractive. I have always tried to run a tight ship in the classroom, and I'm sure the demeanor I projected sometimes veered to the too-serious side of the line. But it has always seemed to me safer to be on that side, especially since I have heard many stories of young women professors whose teaching careers were jeopardized by the difficulties they had in maintaining classroom order.

Scholarship

"Publish or perish" is the general rule in most law schools, just as it is in other parts of academia. Scholarship is certainly the most difficult part of a law professor's job: It is lonely, demanding, and fraught with the risk of failure. Still, for me and most of my colleagues, the opportunity to do scholarly research provides the principal attraction of academic life.

Good legal scholarship is not related to gender. Women are as endowed with the relevant talents—mental discipline, capacity for critical reflection, ability to research and analyze problems, and abstract thought—as are men. If my own scholarship is lacking in merit, it is not because I don't have a man's brain.

Yet I must admit that my sex has had an impact on my scholarship in two real but subtle ways. First, I am not just a woman, I am also a mother; and for several years, I was a single mother. What flowed inexorably from this fact were unavoidable demands on my time and energy. Scholarship also requires time and energy, and the less of either you are able to devote to it, the less scholarship you will produce. It's as simple as that. The faculty here at Virginia understood the realities of my situation and took them into account when setting the timetable for my tenure decision: I was given an extra year. In other words, they gave me "special consideration" in the tenure process because I am a woman. But I like to think that the standard which they ultimately applied to judge the quality of my work was not relaxed. I would find it hard to live with the notion that it was.

The other way in which being a woman has had an impact on my scholarship stems from my very female tendency to doubt whether what I have to say could possibly be of interest to anybody. It may not be that self-doubt is the sole province of women, but women do seem more prone to it than men. And what a debilitating effect it can have! It has been a drain on my emotional energy and has distracted me from concentrating on concerns that really matter. I could not think clearly about a legal problem when at the same time I was trying to convince myself that it was not preposterous for me to be trying. To think well and write coherently, you have to put such destructive worrying aside.

Collegiality

An enormous variety of activities come under the heading collegiality. Some of them are difficult chores such as serving on faculty committees. Others, such as talking with or advising students about non-classroom related topics, hardly seem like work at all. And still others are hardly "activities" in their own right since they are so integral a part of daily life—the conversations in the hall and at lunch, the cups of coffee in the faculty lounge, the continuous exchange of ideas and of gossip about law school life.

The fact that I am a woman has affected my collegial experience more than it has any other aspect of my job. This may be because I have been the only tenured woman on my faculty. Naturally, I have sometimes felt rather isolated. I have not only had to define my *own* particular place in the institution, but by dint of my solitary presence I have fulfilled a representative function for women generally. I realize, as do my colleagues, that I can't represent or speak for the entire female population. But sometimes issues do arise which are framed as "women's issues," and it seems that I am consulted on these as though I had some unique competence to resolve them—not because I have good judgment or keen insight but because I am a woman.

But the reason why being a woman has colored my experience more in the area of "collegiality" than in teaching and scholarship goes deeper than this. The fact is that threading my way into the whole fabric of a predominantly male institution has proved to be a more delicate and complex task than I could have imagined. I have discovered unexpected depths of ambivalence both in myself and in my colleagues' reactions to me, and the process of learning how to work together as equals has been subtle and slow. I can give a couple of reasons why I think this is so: men's typically polite deference to women and women's general concern over maintaining their femininity.

To begin describing the first, I will tell you about an experience I had when I arrived in Virginia, with my two children, to teach for a year as a visiting professor. The dean of the law school at that time was a big, burly, warm-hearted and tough-minded man. I never had any doubts that if I were to succeed at Virginia I would have to convince him that I was a competent teacher and a serious scholar. And yet, one morning as my boys and I were unpacking and settling into our rented house, having arrived less than 48 hours earlier, the doorbell rang. There stood the dean himself, holding an enormous bouquet of flowers. I'd never met him in person before, though we'd spoken on the phone. He'd come because he wanted to welcome me—not just in person but with flowers. In addition, he'd scheduled a coffee and doughnuts gathering in the faculty lounge for the next morning so that everyone could come and meet me.

All of this was very nice and very generous and very kind. I was touched by the warmth and I appreciated the welcome. But I was a little nonplussed to discover that *no other* visiting member of the faculty had ever been welcomed with flowers and a personal visit from the dean, and never before had there been treats for all just because a visitor had arrived. What was I to make of these chivalrous gestures? I couldn't help but wonder what they implied about my new colleagues' expectations of me.

I have noticed these chivalrous inclinations on other occasions too.

For example, since my arrival, the law school has considered a number of applicants for teaching positions. Serious candidates are invited to spend a day at the law school, during which time they proceed through a series of interviews with present faculty members. These sessions—each held in individual faculty offices and attended by the applicant and four or five of our law professors—help us judge the quality of the applicant's mind through discussion of legal issues. The sessions can get pretty lively and very intense. I have the definite but uneasy impression that women applicants have been treated more gently than have the men in these interviews: The questions asked of the women have been less probing, and their answers treated with less skepticism. In short, I think the women candidate's willingness and capacity for intense intellectual debate has been less rigorously challenged.

Occasionally, I have attempted to press female candidates harder than have my male colleagues, but have ended up making *everybody* uncomfortable: the candidate because she was already in a stressful situation and here was I, her natural ally, becoming the aggressor; my colleagues because they were particularly uneasy with her stress and didn't like to see her made even more uncomfortable; and myself because I was breaking some implicit rule about how we go about the process of interviewing female faculty applicants.

I describe this because, although I never went through the interviewing process myself, I feel that I, too, have been the beneficiary of a considerable amount of unearned deference, simply because my colleagues were uncomfortable engaging me in vigorous debate. They're nicer to me when they think I'm wrong than they are to each other.

Of course I have had a role to play in this charade as well, considering that I am also uneasy with the notion that debate and argument —vivid, forceful, intense argument—is an acceptable mode of behavior for *me* as a woman. I am, I think, more argumentative than many women. Indeed, throughout my life I have had difficulty supressing my urge to convince others of my views by argument. But argument and debate are not the customary—nor are they socially acceptable —forms of persuasion for women, and when I become too adversarial or persuasive in discussions I can't help but notice how quickly it begins to feel as though I'd done something inappropriate in coming on so strong.

But then my sense of self was formed during a time when women were not generally valued for their ability to make a contribution in professional terms. I resisted the notion that there were things I couldn't do just because I was a girl, but however much I resisted sex role stereotypes, I was, after all, pretty much like most people in that I basically tried to behave in ways that would earn approval rather than scorn. I learned that I would encounter less resistance to what I really wanted to do if I could retain my femininity in the process. I remember my father when I talked with him about going to law school. He claimed to be enthusiastic about my decision, yet he said to me, "I hope you don't turn out to be like all the lady lawyers I've known. None of them are really ladies. And please, Lil, whatever you do, don't start smoking cigars!" It would have taken a much stronger will than I possessed to have been able to ignore completely his not-too-subtle message.

At this point in my life, it's not a question of lack of will, because I *like* being a woman and I want to retain for myself much of what that traditionally has entailed. I'd rather be a wife than a husband, a mother than a father, the nurturer of my children and not the disciplinarian. I'd rather do the cooking than the plumbing. In other words, even though I do want to do some of the things that were traditionally for men, I never have and never will want to be one of the boys.

It is probably easy to see that my goals occasionally seem self-contradictory, even to me, and on dark days I am plagued by ambivalence. But it is the bright side of things that should emerge from this account. A law professor's job seems to me, on balance, to be practically perfect. It's intellectually stimulating and emotionally challenging and you get the summer off.

CHAPTER 14

AS LAW STUDENT:
Drawings on the Bathroom Wall

BY BARBARA MOSES

Carol W. Moses

BARBARA MOSES

BARBARA MOSES

Orrick, Herrington & Sutcliffe, P.C.
San Francisco, Calif.

Education

J.D., Harvard Law School, 1982, cum laude; Women's Law Association; Articles Editor, *Harvard Journal on Legislation*

B.A., Dartmouth College, 1978, magna cum laude (philosophy)

Experience

Associate, Orrick, Herrington & Sutcliffe, P.C., San Francisco, Calif., 1983-present

Law Clerk to Chief Justice Vincent L. McKusick, Maine Supreme Judicial Court, 1982-1983

Summer Clerk, Hanson, Bridgett, Marcus, Vlahos & Stromberg, San Francisco, Calif., 1982

Summer Clerk, Orrick, Herrington & Sutcliffe, P.C., San Francisco, Calif., 1981

Staff Reporter, Legal Times of Washington, Washington, D.C., summer, 1980

Part-time Newswriter/Reporter, WEEI Radio, Boston, Mass., 1979-1981

Reporter/Anchor, WLOB Radio, Portland, Maine, 1979

Reporter/Anchor, WWNH Radio, Rochester, N.H., 1978-1979

Personal

Born: February 11, 1957, Washington, D.C.
Single

Chapter 14

AS LAW STUDENT: DRAWINGS ON THE BATHROOM WALL

BY BARBARA MOSES

When I first arrived at Harvard Law School, I didn't expect to find any sex discrimination. And for some time after I matriculated, I continued to believe that there wasn't any. I had enrolled in law school in the fall of 1979, after a year and a half working as a radio reporter in small New England towns. Before that, I attended Dartmouth College in New Hampshire.

At Dartmouth, female students were routinely referred to as quahogs (pronounced co-hogs) rather than coeds. A quahog is a large New England clam, too tough for anything but soups and chowders. At Dartmouth, throughout the years I was there, the male-to-female ratio was kept at three-to-one, the result of a compromise entered into between the administration and the alumni during the battle over coeducation. The male students hung banners out their dormitory windows in the fall—just as the new crop of freshmen arrived—reading "Broads Go Home."

I hadn't found the working world—the Real World, as students everywhere call it—much gentler. I grew tired of being asked when on reporting assignments, "What's a nice girl like you doing in a place like this?" I heard it from cops, businessmen, and local government officials. I grew tired of being told that I couldn't hire another woman to work with me at the station because we needed a male voice, or that I wasn't going to be hired to fill an on-air position for the same reason. I grew so tired of it that I went to law school.

I thought I had left sexism behind. For the first few months of law school, I found it hard to take seriously the complaints of other women students. For my first few breaths, the atmosphere at Harvard and in Cambridge felt like fresh air after the overt sexism I had become accustomed to in college and on the job.

But I began to realize that it was only the crudest, most blatant sexism that I escaped, and that I had exchanged it for a subtler, more sophisticated brand. By the time I got to law school, women were no longer oddities in the classroom. We weren't stared at in the hall or in the bookstore; we weren't asked whose wife or girl friend we were at parties. Professors no longer set aside a special "ladies day" each term for calling on their few female students to recite. There was no official quota system to keep down the number of women students. (In fact, Molly Geraghty, Harvard's director of admissions, has said, "I suppose that each [admissions committee] member may (for a variety of reasons) give a small tilt to women applicants.") And no one called us girls.

Because of the absence of overt, shameless prejudice against women, it took me some time to discover the larger, more elusive problems still facing women at Harvard. These residual problems are in some ways more pernicious and far more difficult to tackle than the undisguised chauvinism which greeted earlier women law students. Today's problems are deep-rooted and stubborn. They stem from two centuries of male tradition at the law school: a system built by and for males, geared to a world in which men are the breadwinners and women are the bread-bakers; a university community dominated by men born and raised before the first woman set foot in the law school as a student (women were not allowed to apply for admission until 1950); and a faculty and student body that has learned not to say women aren't meant to be lawyers, but hasn't learned not to think it.

This setting gives rise to four distinct groups of tangible problems for female law students. First, there are blind systematic barriers preventing women from attending and succeeding in law school in large numbers. Second, women are harassed and pressured every day in law school by countless tiny incidents of sex prejudice, trivial in themselves but oppressive in the aggregate. Third, going to law school subjects many women to unexpected personal pressures—

coming from outside the university community—which are never experienced by men. Finally, the psychological aftereffects of deep societal sexism are keeping many women in law school from banding together for support and strength.

Systematic Barriers

Harvard Law School is officially sex-blind. Sex is supposed to play no part in admissions decisions, financial aid, academic life, or the job placement process. Women are treated exactly like men—and that is precisely the problem. All of the rules and guidelines governing admissions, financial aid, academics, and placement were instituted years ago with Harvard's typical law student in mind. Unfortunately, Harvard's typical law student was a white man, either single, or married to a nonprofessional wife. The backgrounds, achievements, concerns, and needs of Harvard's women students are different from those of their male counterparts. As a result, the system doesn't work as well for women as it does for men.

For example, the admissions office uses a number-crunching formula that, I suspect, works to the detriment of female applicants. Each applicant is assigned an "admissions index," or AI, which can determine whether that applicant is ultimately accepted. The AI is a combination of college grades and LSAT scores. An applicant's undergraduate grade-point average is "adjusted" by the admissions office before it is fed into the AI calculation. The adjustment, according to an article published in the *Harvard Law School Bulletin* in 1979, "is based upon a statistical procedure that compares the first-year Harvard Law School performance of Harvard College graduates with that of graduates from other schools and groups of schools." In other words, a 4.0 average from a school whose graduates have traditionally done well at the law school is better than a 4.0 average from a school whose graduates have done poorly at the law school in the past. Although the admissions office does not make public the specific discounts used for specific schools, it is logical to suppose that grade-point averages for graduates of women's colleges are disproportionately downgraded. After all, women comprised a tiny fraction of the law school student body until very recently, and—also until very recently—were subjected to continual ridicule and abuse once they enrolled. Not surprisingly, these women, many of whom were graduates of single-sex colleges, tended not to be shining academic stars. Today, their "failures" are reflected in the discount assigned to the grades of younger women applying to Harvard from the same schools.

Child care and financial aid are two more examples of ways in which a system sex-blind in intent is sexually discriminatory in effect. A woman law student is much more likely to need help arranging child care than is a man. If she's married, odds are that her husband has a full-time job and can't—or won't—take day-to-day responsibility for the kids. A married man, on the other hand, is more likely to have a nonworking wife willing and able to take on that burden. If the woman is divorced, she usually has custody of the children and, therefore, daily responsibility for their welfare. A divorced man, on the other hand, typically has charge of the kids only on weekends or during school vacations. Because Harvard Law School provides only minimal help to students with child care needs, its women students suffer most.

Similarly, a woman is more likely than a man to need financial aid, but is no more likely to qualify. Parents are still more reluctant to pay for a daughter's legal education than for a son's. Even if a woman had a job before entering law school, her earning power was probably less than a man's, so she acquired fewer resources. Harvard takes parental income into account when calculating financial need, no matter how old the student is or how little the parents will actually contribute to their child's education.

None of these inequalities is the fault of the law school in the sense that none was intended to make life tougher for women or to give men an edge. Yet all of them are the law school's responsibility, insofar as the school has any duty to ensure that one group of students is not systematically and effectively disadvantaged by university policies.

"Trivial" Harassment

It's the little things that get to you. The women's bathrooms are inconveniently located afterthoughts. The portraits ringing the library reading room and arrayed throughout the halls and classrooms are all of men—elderly white men. Male professors—and almost all of the professors are male—call out "Mister So-and-So" when they are working from a seating chart without first names or photos. Some call all of their women students "Miss" unless they are corrected. Many, my friends and I agree, don't seem inclined to call on women at all, or have less patience with a woman's stumbling response to a question than they would with a man's.

Once, working late at night in one of the student journal offices, I ducked into a deserted nearby men's room rather than trot to the other end of the hall to reach the women's bathroom. Scrawled on the wall of my stall I found a detailed, full-length nude portrait of a woman labeled "the average HLS coed." Her identifying features were prominently displayed and marked with arrows: "hairy legs," "pimples," "pubic lice," "inadequate tits." The picture had obviously been there for some time; comments had been added in several different handwritings, some of them undoubtedly recent. I was astounded. I could not think who among my male classmates—men who were always careful to say "woman" instead of "girl," men who would never dare opine publicly that a woman's place is in the home or that women are unreliable because they are at the mercy of raging hormones—harbored such deep misogynistic feelings. Worse yet, I could not believe that no one who had used that stall over the past few weeks or months had bothered to wipe the cartoon off, or even to scratch a dissent or reprimand on the wall. I think of the picture in that toilet stall whenever I am tempted to believe that men of my generation have come a long way.

None of the discriminatory incidents marking women's daily life at Harvard is devastating or terrifically burdensome in and of itself. But they add up. And, to make matters worse, the triviality of each component gripe makes it very difficult to convince anyone not the object of these onslaughts—any man, that is—that they are worth correcting. The Harvard Women's Law Association held a meeting with the current law school dean shortly before he took office. When he asked us about the problems we perceived for women at the law school, we began, falteringly, to describe some of our daily trials and tribulations. The time Professor So-and-So made a sexist joke. The graffitti that kept appearing on the Women's Law Association bulletin board. The way a certain instructor had of ignoring "feminist" questions or comments in class. The dean had a rational response to each example. Why didn't you speak with the professor after class? Surely you can keep a closer eye on the bulletin board, or write a letter to the editor of the student newspaper? I could see a look of bewilderment creep across the dean's face. He just didn't understand how any of the things we mentioned could be a big problem. And he was right. But while a drop of water has no perceptible effect on a rock, a steady stream, over time, will wear a boulder away to a pebble.

To compound the difficulty of making men understand the dimension of the problems women face at law school, there is a tendency among many women to keep silent. Most of us have seen that look of bewilderment on enough faces so that we despair of ever getting the point across. Sometimes it's easier just to shut up. Moreover, some women are afraid that complaints seen as trivial will not be merely ignored but actually will be used against us. We don't want to give anyone an opening to remark that women just can't take it, that we are too thin-skinned, that we can't fight our own battles. What these critics don't understand is that we are more than willing to fight our own battles, but that it is their hearts and minds that we are fighting for, and that when we make them aware of the issues, we will be well on our way to winning the war.

Extracurricular Pressure

It is not only the hearts and minds of the men at Harvard Law School that we have to worry about. If the ingrained biases of professors and fellow students were all that we had to deal with, our task would be relatively simple. Unfortunately, law students have parents, friends, and husbands to deal with as well—not to mention the ghosts of sexism past that live in our psyches and trip us up constantly.

For many women, going to law school means risking important personal and family ties. Mothers and fathers still ask their daughters when they're going to give up this law school nonsense and settle down to raise a family. Husbands still ask their wives the same question—more often than I would have guessed. To put it bluntly: Law school is hazardous to a woman's marriage. I don't know what the statistics are on this—or even whether they've ever been compiled—but I have seen an awful lot of women enter law school married and graduate from law school divorced. My friends and I have tried to figure out why this is so. Our best hypothesis is both simple and depressing. A man who has married a woman he thought was his intellectual or professional inferior resents it when she shows him up. The woman who used to depend on her husband's financial acumen—real or imagined—suddenly becomes an expert on tax shelters. The woman who used to support him psychologically through his career challenges is suddenly being flown all over the country by law firms dying to hire her. The woman who used to work at a low-paying job to help make ends meet is suddenly able to support both of them handsomely. Very few men of my generation will admit—none out loud, and few to themselves—that they want wives who look up to them. But I remain convinced that most of them are uneasy with anything else.

I do not mean to say that in all mid-law school divorces the woman is the victim of rampant male chauvinism. There are certainly other reasons why so many marriages fall apart between matriculation and graduation. Sometimes it is the wife who wakes up in the middle of her second year and decides that she wants out. My friend Chris divorced her husband while she was in law school. She says, in retrospect, that her divorce was inevitable, but that her law school experience accelerated the process. For one thing, she says, law school opens up a whole new chapter in a woman's life. She is forced to reevaluate her goals, her choices, her options. She takes a long look at herself and asks where she wants to go and what she wants to do. She may discover, in this self-reckoning process, that what she wants is not what her husband wants, that her path is not her husband's path. Making a related point, Chris says that three years of law school can change a woman's self-image radically. She develops more professional and intellectual self-confidence, and is encouraged to take her needs and aspirations seriously. Psychologically, she becomes more able to stand on her own feet, to face the world alone. If she had gotten married or stayed married partly out of a sense of helplessness, a need for guidance, her marriage may become a prop she no longer requires. Finally, according to Chris, there is the simple fact that law school is a stress-producing experience. It alters a woman's life dramatically, and therefore alters her husband's life as well. The couple may have to move. Their finances may be strained. Their domestic responsibilities may have to be rearranged. Their schedules may no longer mesh—in fact, the wife's is liable to change every semester, and perhaps every week. Sometimes, in a shaky marriage, domestic predictability, routine, habit, keep the couple from seriously questioning their commitment to each other and to their marriage. Once wrenched from the comforts of this superficial tranquility, they may be unable to avoid asking themselves why they should remain married.

To say that a marriage had never been a good one, though, or to say that a marriage inevitably went sour when the wife began to take herself seriously, is not to say that a divorce is easy. Divorce is never easy, and a woman whose divorce is linked to her legal career cannot avoid souring somewhat on the law. It kind of takes the fun out of law school when a woman realizes that its rewards cannot be reaped unless she is willing to risk her marriage.

Psychological Aftereffects

In my third year of law school, I participated in a clinical program, representing indigent criminal defendants in a local district court. One of the judges there was a middle-aged woman. She had gone to law school when women had to fight blatant discrimination at every step of the way. She had made it in a world where most women didn't even try. And she was notorious for her dislike of younger female lawyers. No woman wanted to try a case before her against a male prosecutor.

The roots of this judge's bias were not all that hard to figure out. We—the young woman lawyers and law students appearing in her court—had advantages she had never had. We hadn't faced the formidable obstacles she had overcome. And she resented us for it. She had done it the hard way. She had made it as a woman in a man's world. To see that world changing, to see us breeze along, taking our comparative privileges for granted, took away some of the glory of her achievement.

On a much reduced scale, I think some of the same resentment has operated to keep women apart from each other at law school. Most of us were oddities in high school or college. We had gotten to law school by acting differently from other females we grew up with. More precisely, we had gotten to law school by acting like men. Most of us had been praised at one time or another—and it was intended and accepted as praise—by being told, "You think like a man." Thinking like a man was better than thinking like a woman. And it was special—it set us apart from other girls, who thought like girls. Naturally, many of us wanted to hang on to that feeling of being special. Many of us still think—I should say still feel, as we are all smart enough not to think it consciously—that the best way to prove our worth is to act like men. Hence, it is difficult to involve law school women in a feminist community. To become part of a women's group or project is to admit to being just one of the girls. (Incidentally, I think this is related to the problem many women lawyers have dealing with their female secretaries. A man who goes out to lunch with his secretary and discusses office problems is seen as sensitive and caring. A woman is afraid that if she does the same things she will be perceived as non-executive. Someone might even—horrors!—mistake her for a secretary herself.)

Unwillingness to give up badges of achievement explicitly measured against a male standard leads to unwillingness to question that standard. A woman who has been praised and rewarded for acting like a man has no incentive to ask whether it is good to act like a man—whether either men or women should act like men have always acted. Thus, women in law school tend to accept the law school's traditional scheme of values. Historically, that scheme has placed a premium on a very narrow measure of worth—a student's ability to absorb information, digest it, and spit it out again over a two-hour period in an examination bluebook.

Although all of the women at Harvard Law are tolerably good exam-takers—that's how we got in in the first place—the fact remains that women do not do as well as men academically. Students at Harvard are not ranked within their classes, but I was able to form a rough picture of women's academic performances by going through recent commencement booklets and counting the number of women (judging sex by first name) graduating with honors. My results:

- In 1978, 21 percent of the graduates were women, 15 percent of the cum laude graduates were women, and 13 percent of the magna cum laude graduates were women.
- In 1979, 25 percent of the graduates were women, 23 percent of the cum laude graduates were women, and 10 percent of the magna cum laude graduates were women.
- In 1980, 27 percent of the graduates were women, 20 percent of the cum laude graduates were women, and 8 percent of the magna cum laude graduates were women.

In my graduating class, 30 percent of the class was female, 30 percent of the cum laude graduates were women, and 12 percent of the magna cum laude graduates were women. There was one summa cum laude graduate in my class—a man. Of the 40 members of my class who made the law review, four were women.

The numbers do not upset me, in and of themselves. It takes a certain single-minded devotion to the books to achieve academic distinction at Harvard, and I had always admired those among my classmates who felt that their nonacademic interests and commitments were important enough to stick with, at the cost of a few Latin syllables on their diplomas. None of us was stupid; it was just that our priorities differed. I had always assumed that if women got lower grades than men, on average, it was largely because we were saner, on average. But not everyone saw it that way.

I remember a lunch-table discussion with one of my more venerable law professors. He was very concerned about the scanty representation of women on the law review. He had thought up a number of possible explanations. Perhaps women students entered the law school less well-prepared than their male counterparts. Maybe they were more prone to exam hysteria. It could be that women were more likely to be saddled with household chores and domestic responsibilities than men, thus having less time to study. All of these are reasonable hypotheses; each has some truth. But it never occurred to this professor to question the validity of his twin premises: that grades were the primary measure of success at law school and that each student's goal should be to get the highest grades possible.

I think that some women at the law school share this professor's tunnel vision. And I think it's a shame. I believe that women will have succeeded at the law school not when we achieve mastery over the system on its own terms, but when we achieve enough mastery over ourselves to make the system over, at least partially, in our own image.

CHAPTER 15

A LAWYER-SOCIOLOGIST'S VIEW ON WOMEN'S PROGRESS IN THE PROFESSION

BY DONNA FOSSUM

Julie Wiatt

DONNA FOSSUM

DONNA FOSSUM

Committee on Government Operations
U.S. House of Representatives
Washington, D.C.

Education

Ph.D., State University of New York at Buffalo, 1981 (sociology)

J.D., State University of New York at Buffalo, 1975; Student Editor, *Law and Society Review,* 1972-1975

M.A., State University of New York at Buffalo, 1974 (sociology)

B.A., University of New Mexico, 1971; Phi Beta Kappa, Phi Kappa Phi (anthropology and sociology)

Experience

Professional Staff Member, U.S. House of Representatives, Committee on Government Operations, 1981-present

Fellow, Baldy Center for Law and Social Policy, Buffalo, N.Y., 1980-1981

Research Attorney, American Bar Foundation, Chicago, Ill., 1975-1980

Professional Activities

Admitted to practice in New York, 1976; *in Illinois,* 1976; *in the District of Columbia,* 1978

Member of Advisory Board, Legal Advocacy Fund, American Association of University Women, 1981-present

Consultant and Member, Advisory Committee on Women on Law Faculties Study, American Bar Association, 1979-1980

Consultant, Special Committee on Law School Accreditation, U.S. Office of Education, Department of Health, Education and Welfare, 1977

Member, American Association of University Women; American Bar Association; American Society of Criminology; American Sociological Association; Law and Society Association

Publications

Book Review: *Love Canal: Science, Politics and People, American Bar Association Journal,* Vol. 68 (May 1982)

Women in the Legal Profession: A Study of Social Change, Ph.D. dissertation, SUNY at Buffalo, 1981

"Women in the Legal Profession: A Progress Report" *American Bar Association Journal,* Vol. 67 (May 1981)

"Women Law Professors," *American Bar Foundation Research Journal,* Vol. 1980, No. 4 (1980)

"Law Professors: A Profile of the Teaching Branch of the Legal Profession," *American Bar Foundation Research Journal,* Vol. No. 3, (1980)

"Law School Accreditation Standards and the Structure of American Legal Education," *American Bar Foundation Research Journal,* Vol. 1978, No. 3 (1978)

"An Evaluation of PILOT 100: The Buffalo Police Ride-Along Project," Master's Thesis, SUNY at Buffalo, 1973

"Police-Student Attitudes and Attitude Perceptions of Each Other," *Law and Order,* Vol. 20, No. 4 (1972)

Personal

Born: February 5, 1949, Cedar Rapids, Iowa
Single

Chapter 15

A LAWYER-SOCIOLOGIST'S VIEW ON WOMEN'S PROGRESS IN THE PROFESSION

BY DONNA FOSSUM

Even the most imaginative observer would probably be forced to admit that as lawyers' careers go, mine, which has focused heavily on social science research, has been rather unusual. This is undoubtedly due to the fact that I have persistently tried to use my training in both law and sociology. At times, trying to combine the two disciplines has been difficult, for in a very fundamental respect, they are polar opposites. That is, law stresses the making of distinctions, while sociology emphasizes the finding of commonalities. My dual training has been most valuable, however, in helping me to understand the milieu in which I have been operating since entering the legal profession.

As with virtually all women lawyers, I have first-hand knowledge of the triumphs and mishaps of law school, bar examinations, and work, but unlike the rest, I have made it a professional priority to attempt to put my experiences in their larger social context. In so doing, I have discovered that my development as a lawyer closely parallels the sexual integration of the legal profession. Exploring the ramifications of this social change has provided me with valuable insights into my own career experiences and has given me what I suspect is a rather unusual perspective on what it is like to be a woman in the legal profession. I can illustrate by describing a few of my experiences.

When I began law school in the fall of 1972, I had no idea that I was entering hostile territory. The first inkling of that came in my contracts class when I encountered the doctrine of coverture.

I do not remember the exact name of the case in which the doctrine was presented, but I do remember that I spent more than the usual time studying it. I was sure that I had to be misreading the case, for it seemed to be telling me that the doctrine was the principle whereby women who married ceased to exist in the eyes of the law. This could not be! Husbands do not own their wives! Women are not property!

I remember reading the case over and over again and finally going to the library to find out how I could have gone so wrong. It was there that I came across Blackstone's statement on coverture in which he described how when a man and a woman marry they become one, and that one is the husband. I had not been wrong about the meaning of the doctrine. What was wrong, was the doctrine itself!

Even though I quickly ascertained that only a few vestiges of the doctrine remained, I was left with a sense of personal violation. Somehow the law was not turning out to be what I thought it was. It seemed to be more concerned with order than with justice. As a woman, I was not finding the law to be very friendly. Indeed, it appeared that it might be my enemy.

As the semester progressed, my suspicion of the law grew to encompass many of the members of the legal profession. I became painfully aware of the fact that several of my professors (all of whom were male) called on the women in my classes much more frequently than the men. In a Socratic setting this meant that a student (i.e., legal amateur) was expected to hold her own in a high-speed, extemporaneous verbal joust with a professor (i.e., legal professional). The result of this encounter was frequently total humiliation on the part of the student. At first, I attributed this practice to blatant discrimination. After a time, however, it occurred to me that the professors did this because it was much easier to learn women's names as there were so few of us—only 42 in a class of 176. I was absolutely shocked to discover that the women in my first-year class accounted for almost 50 percent of the total female enrollment in the law school, since there were only 29 women in the second year class and 18 in the third. In all, we comprised only 16 percent of the law school's student body.

Halfway through the first semester of law school, I concluded that the treatment of women by the law and the role of women in the legal profession were closely related and that both were most disturbing. It was impossible to reach any other conclusion after a debate in criminal law class regarding whether rape should be treated as a special offense or as an ordinary assault. Not surprisingly, more emotion than logic was displayed during much of the debate. Most men argued to keep rape a special crime while most women argued to treat rape like an ordinary assault. The level of emotion rose considerably among the women when it became apparent that many of the men subscribed to the notion that there were only two kinds of women—mothers and prostitutes. To protect sainted mothers (both their own and their children's) from terrible rapists, they felt it was necessary to make rape a special crime. To protect honorable men like themselves from all the conniving prostitutes, however, proof of rape required more evidence than proof of an ordinary assault. Regardless of how effectively we women argued, it was clear that the men would prevail in our classroom; they outnumbered us three to one. The feeling of powerlessness was enraging.

When second semester began, there was but one topic of discussion—*Roe v. Wade,* the decision just handed down by the Supreme Court legalizing abortion. I had at least one friend who had had an abortion. So did several others in class. The notion that, in doing so, our friends were criminals had never really registered until the court decision said so. This realization was necessarily most bothersome. Most of the men in class either strongly favored or strongly opposed the decriminalization of abortion. Some saw it simply as an alternative to "the Pill," while others saw it as murder. For the women it was not that easy to define. I was glad that I finally had the right to choose, but I resented the fact that I had needed the permission of men to obtain dominion over my own body.

The more I studied the law, the more I learned about my legal disabilities as a woman. For most of the men in class, the cases that touched on women's legal status were just more court decisions they had to read and digest. For me, these cases were not just part of the ordinary curriculum—they were the sum total of a very personal education and enlightenment. I suspect that the effect upon me of reading these cases was similar to the effect upon black students when reading cases on slavery. They made me angry and more determined to succeed in law school. They also dashed my illusions about the synonymity of law and justice. By the end of the second year of law school, the naive faith that I had had in the innate rightness of the law and its practitioners was gone. It had been replaced with a feeling of distrust and suspicion, colored by the conviction that things had to be corrected.

By the third year of law school, I knew that to succeed in law school, it was necessary to forsake much of my basic feminine socialization: I had discovered that "thinking like a lawyer" all too often meant "thinking like a man." The internal conflict this generated in women was very real, but rarely articulated. It appeared to take its toll, however, for only about 80 percent of the women who started law school with me in 1972 graduated with me in 1975, whereas close to 100 percent of the men did. Several years later it came as no surprise when I read the results of a study in the *Journal of Legal Education* which found that "successful female law students showed fairly consistent cross-sex identification" in that "they described themselves in terms usually applied to males" and "rejected more feminine characterizations." Somehow the denial of one's femininity seemed to be an awfully high price to pay for successful entry into a profession.

Third-year law students have traditionally been less oriented toward their studies than toward their future employment. My fellow classmates were no exception. Job interviews began shortly after classes started in the fall and continued well into second semester. Unprecedented numbers of suits, chins, and ears appeared in class, and lunch hour debates on holdings were replaced with discussions of job offers.

Making the leap from law student to lawyer seemed to be more difficult for the women than for the men. I suspect that this was at least partly due to the fact that it was the first time that all of us were forced to address the potential conflict between effectively serving others as attorneys and making good livings for ourselves. For the men, there was no conflict; they were overwhelmingly concerned with making a good living. For a disproportionate number of the women, however, there was a conflict; they wanted to do both. The realization that they might not be able to do so came as a shock and a disappointment. I later learned, through research presented at the 1977 annual meeting of the American Sociological Association, that this general difference in professional orientation between men and women law students had been empirically confirmed; but even if we had known that others suffered the same conflict, it would have provided little consolation.

I was luckier than most of my classmates, for I had decided to pursue a career in research and consequently was spared the ordeal of interviewing for a job with assorted law firms, corporations, and government agencies. As their friend and confidant, however, I daily shared the details of each and every interview. In listening to the accounts of their interviews, some notable differences between the experiences of my male and female friends became apparent. The women were much more likely than the men to be asked the intimate details of their personal lives. Prospective employers might understandably want to know about their plans to have children, but I suspect that there was a better way to elicit this information than asking, "Are you on 'the Pill'?" Not surprisingly, several of the women were flabbergasted by such an approach. In addition, a couple of the women who were married to attorneys in private practice, were informed, when this fact came out in interviews with law firms, that they would have to look for jobs in the public sector because no respectable law firm would hire an attorney who shared a bed with an attorney from another law firm!

Despite such unpleasant incidents during job interviews, virtually all of the women in my class landed good legal jobs well before graduation. This fact irked a number of the men in class who were having trouble finding employment and who were not afraid to verbalize their view that the only reason the women got their jobs was because of their sex. The fact that the women disproportionately ranked in the top of the class escaped these male students. Fortunately, this fact was not lost on employers, who in most cases were looking for promising legal talent, as well as their first women attorneys.

As most of my classmates embarked on careers as practicing lawyers, I plunged into the world of research. My specialty quickly became legal education. In the process of studying law school accreditation standards and law professors, I occasionally stumbled across snippets about women in the legal profession. Set forth in a sentence or two, or buried in footnotes, were tidbits about the women who had preceded me in the profession. Although this information had no direct relevance to my ongoing research, I began hoarding it. One day I came across a reference to the fact that the last all-male ABA accredited law school had gone coed in 1972. That was the year that *I* had begun law school! It had never before occurred to me how very recent women's arrival in the legal profession might be. I was stunned to realize that *I* might be in the vanguard of women who were sexually integrating the legal profession.

This discovery had a profound impact on my career, for I became determined to learn everything I could about women in the legal profession. Since my research at the time focused on law professors, I began there. I knew from my own law school experience that women law professors were rare commodities because there had been only one on the faculty when I began law school and only three when I graduated. Nothing had prepared me, however, for what I found when I delved more deeply into the topic.

When I began looking through the faculty rosters of law schools, I was pleasantly surprised to find how many included women as far back as the 1940's and 1950's. Closer examination revealed, however, that most of these women were librarians who did little or no teaching. I also found that as the position of law school librarian became more professionalized and consequently more prestigious, women were replaced by men. When I tabulated the number of women who had actually taught on the regular faculties of law schools, I found that of over 1,200 law professors in 1950, only five had been women, and of over 1,600 in 1960, only 11 had been women. Virtually all of them had taught family law, trusts and estates, or legal research and writing, not exactly the meatiest of law courses. The data were so outrageous that I had to keep reminding myself that they were for years in my own lifetime and not for some previous century.

I discovered that it was not until the years when I was in law school that the number of women law professors began to increase substantially. In 1972, there had been only 129 women law professors, accounting for 3.7 percent of the total. By 1975, these figures had risen to 296 and 6.9 percent respectively. On the average, there had been approximately one woman faculty member per law school in 1972 and approximately two in 1975. Why had there been so few women law professors for so long? Why had their ranks more than doubled in size in the early 1970's? Finding the answers to these questions forced me to expand the scope of my research considerably.

When I explored the status of women in the context of the entire legal profession, I discovered a long history of discrimination. I quickly realized, however, that to get a fair picture, I had to distinguish between the treatment of women by individual male attorneys and their treatment by groups of male attorneys acting in institutional forms such as law schools, legislatures, courts, law firms, and bar associations. Some individual attorneys had been very supportive of women, while most institutional groups had not. Until very recently, the policies and practices of many of these institutions severely restricted the opportunities of women to pursue careers in the legal profession.

Among the first things I came across in my research was the 1873 case of *Bradwell v. Illinois.* In its decision, the U.S. Supreme Court had agreed with the State of Illinois that women could be prevented from practicing law. I thought it interesting that of the myriad cases I had been required to read in law school, this had not been one of them. After reading the case, I was not surprised to learn that it had taken until the turn of the century for women to obtain permission to practice law in most states. Obtaining permission to practice law and actually being able to do so, however, were two very different things. While women had been struggling to gain permission to sit for the bar examinations of the various states, graduation from law school had rapidly become a virtual prerequisite for taking such examinations, and many law schools refused to admit women. Consequently, the next challenge women faced was gaining admittance to the nation's law schools. I was shocked to discover that among the last law schools in the nation to admit women was Harvard. No wonder women had trouble making headway in the legal profession. Until the early 1950's, they had been denied one of the most valuable credentials a lawyer could have—a Harvard law degree.

At the law schools women were allowed to attend, they rarely comprised more than a tiny fraction of the student body. One notable exception was Portia, an all-women law school in Boston that operated between 1908 and 1934. Without a doubt, the discovery of this law school was one of the bright spots in my research. Another was New York University, which had admitted women considerably before many other law schools and had consistently admitted them in far greater numbers. I discovered, however, that for law schools as a group, as recently as 1960, only about 375 women were graduated that year (about 3 percent of the total graduates). Several studies I came across indicated that the low proportion of women students at law schools was attributable to a lack of women applicants. Others contained evidence, however, that it was the result of low quotas for women students and higher admissions standards for women applicants.

The more I learned about the history of women in the legal profession, the more depressed I got. It seemed that women had encountered obstacles almost everywhere conceivable. I found that they had been denied membership in the American Bar Association until 1918. They disproportionately worked in low-prestige specialties and in the back-room areas of law that lacked client contact. And, not surprisingly, they made considerably less money than men. As I compiled figures on the number of women enrolled in law school since World War II, I discovered that it was not until the past decade that women became law students in significant numbers. As I suspected, I was, indeed, part of the vanguard of women who were sexually integrating the legal profession. Why were things different in the 1970's? What had changed? I knew that the answers to these questions would provide me with the last pieces in the puzzle.

Unbeknownst to me and the other women who entered law school in the early 1970's, we were riding the crest of two waves that were destined to have a profound effect on the sexual composition of the nation's law schools. One was the modern women's movement which consciously and unconsciously encouraged young women, like me, to pursue careers in nontraditional professions, such as law. The other was the war in Vietnam, which deprived the nation's law schools of an adequate supply of male students. Although both of these events actually began earlier than the 1970's, the nation's law schools did not really feel their impact until the late 1960's and early 1970's. Between 1969 and 1972, the number of women applying to law school increased fourteen-fold, while the total number of law school applicants only tripled. During this same period, the number of women enrolled in law school increased dramatically from 4,264 to 11,376 or from 7 to 12.2 percent.

I discovered that during this same period, the federal government took two legal actions which had some potential impact on the status of women in the legal profession. One was Executive Order 11375, effective since 1968, which prohibits employment discrimination based on sex by federal contractors. The other was the Higher Education Act of 1972, of which Title IX prohibits sex discrimination in the employment as well as the admissions policies and practices of all higher education institutions receiving federal aid. For decades before the enactment of these laws, the nation's law schools had operated as autonomous communities whose members (i.e., existing faculty and deans) decided whom to admit as students and whom to hire as teachers. With the issuance by the president of Executive Order 11375 and the passage by Congress of the Higher Education Act, however, the policies of almost all law schools suddenly became subject to control by the federal government, because almost all receive federal funds.

Determining the possible impact that these two laws had on the status of women in the legal profession totally consumed several months of my life. Throughout the winter of 1980 and the spring of 1981, I gathered and analyzed all the data I could find that appeared to be relevant. In the end, I concluded that the issuance and, more importantly, the enforcement of Executive Order 11375 had caused most law schools to add women to their regular teaching faculties. The data clearly indicated that in the absence of this order, the percentage of women law faculty at the end of the 1970's would have been about half of what it actually was (i.e., an estimated 5.5 percent of the total compared to 10.5 percent). But I also concluded that the passage of the Higher Education Act had not caused the nation's law schools to admit more women students. The data strongly suggested that several years before the passage of this law, the end of draft deferments and the personnel needs of the U.S. military had robbed most schools of male law students and forced them to admit increased numbers of women to protect their tuition bases. I found it extremely interesting to discover that only once prior to the advent of the Vietnam War had women comprised more than 4 percent of the nation's law students, and that had been for a period of two years during and immediately following the Korean War. It took me a while to absorb the full meaning of these findings, because I did not want to acknowledge the magnitude of the collective resistance to the presence of women that had been displayed over the years by the legal profession. I was forced to conclude that many law schools added women to their faculties only because a law had forced them to do so, and that I had probably been admitted to law school more because I was draft-proof than because I was academically qualified.

When I concluded my research in the spring of 1981, I thought it only fitting that I should try to assess the current status of women in the legal profession. In so doing I discovered that the number of women lawyers had quadrupled during the 1970's and that by the early 1980's they comprised 12 to 13 percent of the profession, a notable improvement over five percent in 1970. Meaningful numbers of women were beginning to appear on the letterheads of law firms, on the faculties of law schools, and on the bench. In 1980, women comprised 22 percent of the associates and two percent of the partners in the 50 largest law firms in the nation. They accounted for 28 percent of the assistant, 17 percent of the associate, and five percent of the full professors at the nation's law schools, a total of almost 11 percent of all professors. In addition, they accounted for almost seven percent of the federal bench.

Despite this progress, studies revealed, however, that women continued to cluster in the back-room and low-prestige areas of law and that they still made significantly less money than men. Within days of completing my research, Sandra Day O'Connor was nominated to serve on the U.S. Supreme Court. The fact that this woman had only 30 years previously found it difficult to find a job after graduating in the top of her law school class, illustrated how very recently women had begun to be accepted as full members of the legal profession.

Judging from a number of the comments made at the time of O'Connor's nomination and confirmation, I was forced to conclude that acceptance of women by the legal profession was still quite grudging. On at least a dozen occasions, prominent male members of law firms, law schools, the bench, and bar associations, who were familiar with my research, asked me if I was satisfied now that a woman was on the Supreme Court. I said, "No, I would not be satisfied until women's representation on the nation's highest court more closely reflected their numbers in the general population." When I estimated that about four more women on the court would satisfy me, mutterings of "hopeless feminist" were frequently heard in reply. These exchanges made me realize that a century after the first women had been admitted to the practice of law in this country, women's appropriate role within the legal profession was all too often considered to be a token one.

I still believe that the gains women have made in recent years in the legal profession are most encouraging. If present trends continue, my data indicate that women will account for half of all law students by 1990 and one-third of all lawyers by 2000. I would be lying, however, if I said that I thought that women's struggle to gain acceptance was over. At its annual meeting in the summer of 1982, the American Bar Association withdrew its endorsement of legislation that sought to eliminate sex discrimination in private clubs that were primarily business clubs in nature. Despite the fact that at least one lawyer who held public office noted that he conducted much of his business and raised most of his campaign funds at his club, the majority of the lawyers present believed that women were not denied opportunities for professional progress by being excluded from such private clubs. Even though the ABA reversed this action and went on record as endorsing the legislation, I was as angered that this endorsement was ever withdrawn as were other women attorneys, but I was not surprised as they were. My research had already convinced me that our status within the profession is far from secure. Unfortunately, even today, women's position within the legal profession, as well as society as a whole, is all too frequently that of visitor rather than member in full standing.